RESTLESS SPIRITS

Allan Havis

BROADWAY PLAY PUBLISHING INC
224 E 62nd St, NY, NY 10065
www.broadwayplaypub.com
info@broadwayplaypub.com

RESTLESS SPIRITS
© Copyright 2006 by Allan Havis

First printing: January 2006
I S B N: 0-88145-302-1

Book design: Marie Donovan
Word processing: Microsoft Word
Typographic controls: Ventura Publisher
Typeface: Palatino
Printed and bound in the U S A

RESTLESS SPIRITS was originally commissioned
and produced by San Diego Repertory Theater
(Sam Woodhouse, Artistic Director; Karen Wood,
Managing Director), opening on 3 February 2006.
The cast and creative contributors were:

JESSIE GORDON . . . . Karole Foreman
FELIX, RUBIO . . . . Kinan Valdez
MOM, TEACHER 3 . . . . Sylvia M'Lafi Thompson
DAD, HAMADI, PROFESSOR . . . . .Wendell W Wright
WINCHESTER . . . . Jim Chovick
BENNY, DIEGO, TEACHER 2 . . . . Raul Cardona
QUEE, TEACHER 1, DOCTOR . . . . April Doctolero
CHANTELLE, JESSIE'S DAUGHTER . . . . . . Bibi Valderrama
SAMANTHA . . . . Zoe Eprile

Director . . . . Sam Woodhouse
Choreographer . . . . Jean Isaacs
Assistant director/Dramaturg . . . . Michael Jaros
Set designer . . . . Robin Roberts
Lighting designer . . . . Jennifer Setlow
Projections designer . . . . Victoria Petrovich
Costume designer . . . . Melanie Watnick
Sound designer . . . . George Ye
Stage manager . . . . Dana Anderson
Assistant stage manager . . . . Meghan Bourdeau
Consulting folklorist . . . . Antone Minard
Casting/Artistic coordinator . . . . Emily Cornelius

Special thanks to San Diego Rep Artistic Director Sam Woodhouse for having the expansive vision, faith, and heart to make RESTLESS SPIRITS come into being.

Thanks for help in the various stages of the script and production:

Community interviews conducted by:
Negeen Mirreghabie
Megan Ma
Maya Gurantz

Resource team and consultants:
Michael Schudson
Yen Le Espiritu
Delicia Turner Sonnenberg
Adelaida R Del Castillo
Al Irvine
Stefan Tanaka
David Avalos
Evelyn Cruz
Peter Cirino
Viviana Acosta
Isidro D Ortiz
Ghada Osman
Margaret Larlham
Paul Strand
Michele Schlecht
Ramona Perez
Michele Schlecht
Nicola Broad
Márgara de León
Oliva M Espin
Joyce M Gattas
Nadine George-Graves
Aglae Saint-Lot

Stefan Tanaka
Elizabeth Yamada
Winston Butler

Regina Marchi
Gideon Rapport
Ross Frank
Viviana Acosta
David Avalos

Joyce M Gattas
Kathy Jones
Lee Ann Kim
Andy Lowe
Marianne Macdonald
Richard Madsen
Nan McDonald
Enrique Morones
Isidro Ortiz
Ghada Osman
John Panter
Ramona Perez
Lewis Peterman
Ian Pumpian
Christina Rivera-Garza
John Rushes
Aglae Saint-Lot
Michele Schlecht
William A Virchis
Elizabeth Yamada

Additional thanks to San Diego State University, San Diego City College, University of California San Diego

RESTLESS SPIRITS was made possible by the following granting agencies:

The Colonel Frank C Wood Memorial Fund, the San Diego Foundation Community Endowment Fund, Reuben H Fleet Foundation Discretionary Fund and the Arts & Culture Grant Program Fund at the San Diego Foundation. The California Council For the Humanities as part of the Council's statewide California Stories Initiative. The James Irvine Foundation First Decade Project.

The Kerr Endowment; University of California, San Diego research grant.

The National Endowment For the Arts, Access To Artistic Excellence Program.

CHARACTERS & SETTING

TEACHERS 1, 2 & 3, *daycare school*
BENNY, *native American, late sixties, tailor—always has hat on*
JESSIE, *PhD candidate, late thirties, black female with high drives*
FELIX, *late thirties, Chicano, autodidact elevator inspector*
MOM (JESSIE's), *Mrs Phyllis Gordon, middle aged widow with only one child*
RUBIO, *farm worker, Chicano*
DIEGO, *farm worker, Chicano*
HAMADI, *middle aged African man*
DAVID WINCHESTER, *middle aged white man, indicted child killer*
SAMANTHA, *somewhere between four and six year old girl*
CHANTELLE, *somewhere between four and six year old girl*
DOCTOR TRINA RICHARDS, *O B/G Y N physician intern*
PROFESSOR BLANK
DAD, JESSIE's *ghostly father, Professor Martin Gordon*
QUEE, *second generation Cambodian girl, age eighteen*

(Actor playing a TEACHER *can double to play* MOM*)*
(Actor playing one of the TEACHERS *can also play* DOCTOR*)*
(Actor playing FELIX *can double as* RUBIO*)*
(Actor playing BENNY *can double as* DIEGO*)*
(Actor playing FATHER *can double as* HAMADI*)*

Time: *October/ November 2005 (and 2009 in Epilogue)*

Setting: *Various locations in around San Diego County, Tijuana, Mexico, and the Pacific Ocean*

to my wonderful children, Simone & Julian

ACT ONE

Prologue

(SAMANTHA *is on a park swing in front of a gravestone.*
She holds a puppet or doll perhaps.)

SAMANTHA: My darling teddy bears.
Come out, come out
And drop your silly fears
(Dolls dance)
Teddy bear, Teddy bear
Show your shoe
(Different voice)
Teddy bear, Teddy bear
That will do.
(Normal)
Teddy bear, Teddy bear
Run downstairs
(Different voice)
Teddy bear, Teddy bear
Stop your tears
(Normal)
Teddy bear, Teddy bear,
Turn on the light
(Different voice)
Teddy bear, Teddy bear,
Smile with great delight!

(He takes first phrase. She takes second phrase through text.
He walks toward her. She seeks higher ground—climbing

steps, a ladder, or scaffolding. He holds a red balloon attached to a long string.)

WINCHESTER/SAMANTHA: All the children know
the pied piper gave way,
And soon upon us
is the Wildest Day
All the children know
Great Fires came in October.
Nine months after cold murder.
All the children know
the Van Buren girl still walks.
Chantelle...
Chantelle...
All the children fear Satan
and they hear his footsteps
When no one else can.
There is tapping on the window
And the ceiling buckles and creaks

SAMANTHA: Chantelle, Chantelle...

WINCHESTER/SAMANTHA: Chantelle...

(We see CHANTELLE *in the mist, she might hold a battered doll without toy clothes.)*

WINCHESTER/SAMANTHA: All the children sleep
Bundled up like kittens.
Halloween comes twice this year.
Once for the fat candy merchants
Once more for the embolden ones.
All the young children have
Wonderful fantasy friends.
The door swings both ways
On their tender imagination
Is there one adult willing and ready
who will come to their rescue?

*(*WINCHESTER *lets go of balloon and it sails away.*
SAMANTHA *approaches* CHANTELLE *on the swing and joins*

*her on the second swing. As they pump higher, they giggle
and laugh at* WINCHESTER.)

Scene One

*(A day of the dead ceremony in Tijuana. Silence. Hushed
whispers. Throbbing drums with other folk instruments.
Stage lights are black except for a few candles. We hear
singing from the back of the theater. We see one human figure
without clothes, but sporting a smiling death mask. Lights
rise revealing one or two altars. A processional carrying an
open coffin wends around the stage and audience. We hear
a happy children's choral in Spanish.)*

JESSIE: Good evening. This is the last of the three
lectures on death and the supernatural in pre-industrial
cultures. And I've used my own photos unless
otherwise stated.

*(We see slides and projections throughout the following the
girl with a broom sweeps the gravestone onstage.)*

JESSIE: Every autumn for hundreds of years Monarch
Butterflies return to Mexico for their winter habitat
in the *oyamel* fir trees. These beautiful butterflies have
traveled thousands of miles from Canada. A migration
that appeals to a universal sense of magic. The rural
Mexican people believe the butterflies bear the spirits
of their departed.

*(A skeletal figure rises from inside the open coffin and
cheerfully waves his hand in slow motion. The coffin is
lowered into a grave.)*

JESSIE: Such elusive and festive spirits are honored
during *Dia de los Muertos—The Day of the Dead*. Not to
be confused with The Grateful Dead—a posthumous
rock group.

(WINCHESTER howls softly in the distance.)

JESSIE: *Dia de los Muertos* similar to the rituals of Halloween and Mardi Gras, evolved from the Celts, the Romans, the Aztecs, and Christian practices of All Saints and All Souls Day. We fear not the dead, we laugh and cheat at life, we become invincible for an instant.

(Slides are shown. WINCHESTER *disappears like the Cheshire Cat. we hear the sound of a children's choral in Spanish. The blonde girl—*CHANTELLE*—walks slowly onstage)*

JESSIE: The building of altars not only happens in preparation of *Dia de los Muertos*, but you can see such tributes—marking specific traffic fatalities—along roadways on both sides of the border. You can also find a special altar in east county which honors countless Mexican refugees who have perished in winter looking for an honest day's work.

(Slide of a refugee altar at the entrance to the Coronado Bridge. SAMANTHA *disappears. More slides)*

(She assembles an altar, holding a photo in her hand which we also see on the screen of a distinguished African-American man. We also see a slide of the blonde girl.)

JESSIE: In homes, we find *ofrendas* or "altars" with bread, flowers, candy and fresh fruit. The altars that I have made display my father's cuff links, photos, and cologne.

*(*CHANTELLE *approaches* JESSIE, JESSIE *sees her.)*

(As the woman lights a candle, a man rises in the theater audience CHANTELLE *exits.)*

FELIX: Surely, *the bright civilized folks here* believe in ghosts just like the indigenous people.

JESSIE: Excuse me?

FELIX: *(Stands. charming and sweet)* Your last lecture at this college hinted that we could talk to afterlife spirits.

JESSIE: I'll take questions *at the end of this lecture.*

FELIX: I thought you were done.

JESSIE: Please sit down. Are you one of my students?

FELIX: No, but I want to ask you something.

JESSIE: What is your name?

FELIX: Felix.

JESSIE: *(She shuts down the projections and music.)*
Go ahead, Felix.

FELIX: Why do you deny the various elements in front
of your gorgeous eyes?

(We hear the wondrous sound of birds taking flight.
FELIX *and* JESSIE *look at upward in amazement. We see
a billion monarch butterflies soaring high. Lights flicker
and sparkle. we hear festive music, see balloons in the air.)*

(End of scene)

Scene Two

*(*JESSIE *and her mother at IHOP, on line for a breakfast table.
balloons hover above. Sign says: "Grand Opening. Welcome
to IHOP".)*

VOICEOVER: Munckton party of four. Your table is
ready.

JESSIE: Why do we always meet at IHOP?

MOM: Two for one coupons, baby. They come in the
mail.

JESSIE: Please don't look at me that way.

MOM: What way?

JESSIE: I'm not pregnant.

(Hands her a menu from check-out counter)

MOM: Did I mishear your phone message?

JESSIE: I think so. I said something nice came from the *Stork Foundation*. It was a *grant. To support my research.*

MOM: I believe in *storks...it only takes a little inspiration.*

JESSIE: Sometimes I think you're completely crazy.

MOM: Not completely.

JESSIE: Why obsess about my fertility?

MOM: Well, you have put on a little weight, pumpkin.

(She handles JESSIE *with lightning speed.)*

MOM: Besides I had a very wild dream. A few women were bobbing for apples at a school party and you came out of the water with a very talkative baby clinging to your breast. She spoke in complete iambic sentences and dropped words like paparazzi and gorgonzola.

JESSIE: Very Italian. I thought you don't remember your dreams?

MOM: Only when I sleep in tight spandex with the T V on. The dream was so vivid I wet my bed.

JESSIE: I told you I'm on the pill.

MOM: Which pill?

JESSIE: I can't make it a long breakfast.

MOM: You insisted we meet today.

JESSIE: I'm running low on money.

MOM: Your father set up a trust for you.

JESSIE: Well, it's not enough, Mom. I need five hundred dollars this week.

MOM: What about your grant?

JESSIE: That only covers books and audio visual.

MOM: *(This is a win for her)* Let me take you shopping for clothes after breakfast *and then I'll loan you the cash.*

JESSIE: My dissertation meeting is at eleven.

MOM: Those dunces all have goddamn cell phones.

(JESSIE makes a face.)

MOM: How is it going?

JESSIE: My advisor hates my dissertation idea after approving it. Christ, the entire committee might shaft me.

MOM: Well, I think I'll have the Lingonberry pancakes with a dusting of sugar.

JESSIE: Did you hear what I just said?

MOM: Yes, they don't love you at school like they used too and I'm sure it's the way you dress.

JESSIE: I was the star of my department! Now my committee wants to ground me in ethnic mythology.

MOM: So?

JESSIE: My focus is not *cultural fairy tales!*

MOM: What the heck *is* your focus?

JESSIE: The phenomenology of ghosts within San Diego and Tijuana's immigrant communities.

MOM: Princess, is that worth four years of your young, beautiful life? And that paisley tie does not work with that blouse!

JESSIE: My work's a continuation of Daddy's life thesis.

(Overlapping with the next line)

MOM: I never liked *Annie Hall.*

JESSIE: Mom!

MOM: I know you hate Woody Allen. So when will you have children?

JESSIE: After I secure a *bona fide* ghost.

(One of the balloons pops.)

MOM: *(Aware of her timing with this line)* I think it's time for you to *give up the ghost.*

JESSIE: You talk to Daddy, don't you?

MOM: Sometimes.

JESSIE: Daddy's dead.

MOM: That's my *phenomenology! (Solicitious)* Daddy talks to you?

JESSIE: *(Snacking on Gold Fish crackers)* I met a very charming guy on campus.

MOM: Oh?

JESSIE: Not with the college. He inspects city elevators.

MOM: Are you P M S?

JESSIE: *All the time.* Are you *still* menopausal?

(MOM smiles sweetly.)

JESSIE: He's well read; he's into the occult; he drives an old V W bug painted powder blue.

MOM: Powder blue is a *disastrous* color for you.

JESSIE: And I dreamt about this guy months ago sailing over the Coronado Bridge.

MOM: Darling, you have an undergraduate degree from Yale.

JESSIE: So?

MOM: An elevator operator?

JESSIE: He's *an inspector*—that's middle management.

MOM: What exactly are you telling me, Jessie?

JESSIE: Nothing.

MOM: Then you *are* pregnant, because you don't snack. What is this frog-prince's name?

JESSIE: Felix.

MOM: Felix the Frog?

JESSIE: He has an Irish surname.

MOM: Oh, no.

JESSIE: He looks like Johnny Depp when he made *Pirates of the Caribbean.*

MOM: Fishnet stockings? Mascara?

JESSIE: *(Playful)* With rings and jewelry!

MOM: Honey, I told you a thousand times, stay away from these damn Wal-Mart idiots.

VOICEOVER: Mister and Mrs Saperstein. Your booth is ready.

MOM: Christ, how long do we have to wait for a table!

JESSIE: *(Giving her* MOM *shit)* Felix told me that elevators are not safe. Power outages, cable breaks, snapping doors. Always take the stairs.

MOM: I live on the *goddamn ninth floor.* Want me to rappel down on my garter belt? Where did you meet this clown?

JESSIE: At a lecture I gave a couple of weeks ago.

MOM: So he picked you up?

JESSIE: No. Yes. What difference does it make?

MOM: You tell me!

JESSIE: He has insight on ghosts.

MOM: *(Teasing)* I thought you're not allowed to believe in ghosts?

JESSIE: I'm trying to remain intellectually neutral, Mom.

MOM: Neutral?

JESSIE: Skeptical. That's the only way I can finish my dissertation. Still, Felix has the "shine".

MOM: The "shine"?

JESSIE: Like Daddy. Felix can read minds and sees auras.

MOM: And he has a fat tattoo on his ass?

JESSIE: He told me ghosts like shafts more than graveyards. That's why people have a visceral discomfort inside an elevator.

MOM: Well, I'm really impressed now.

JESSIE: Plus, he's a good dancer...like Daddy.

MOM: Does he know how to smile with *all his teeth*?

JESSIE: *(Broadest of smiles)* Yes.

MOM: Well, I guess I just have to meet Prince Charming.

(End of scene)

Scene Three

(School bell. Outside yard at a day care center in Clairemont Mesa, San Diego)

TEACHER 1: Should we set up for Samantha's birthday?

TEACHER 2: Better now while *the little monsters* are inside.

TEACHER 1: Is the cake in the fridge?

TEACHER 2: It's larger than the fridge.

TEACHER 1: You don't like Samantha's mother, do you?

TEACHER 2: Does it show?

TEACHER 1: Yes. I know Mrs Shepard has venomous fangs.

TEACHER 2: Do you like her?

TEACHER 1: *I like everyone.* Samantha's mom is on some kind of radical diet med and it's making her *mega-schizo-psychotic.*

TEACHER 2: Don't say that, please.

TEACHER 1: Why? It's true.

TEACHER 2: I just don't like that phrase.

TEACHER 1: *(Says the first two "buzz" words rapidly, but stretches "mega".)* Psychotic? Schizo? Or meeeeeeeeeeeega? Mrs Shepard is edgy. That's all it is.

TEACHER 2: Yeah, edgy. Like Courtney Love on uppers

(TEACHER 3 *comes outside.*)

TEACHER 3: Let's bring in everyone early. It's so hot. Are you guys on a break?

TEACHER 2: I'm *never* on a break!

TEACHER 3: Did you send Samantha inside to use the potty?

TEACHER 1: Samantha?

TEACHER 3: Yeah.

TEACHER 1: Samantha never came out here.

TEACHER 3: I sent her outside fifteen minutes ago.

TEACHER 2: I haven't seen her either.

TEACHER 3: O K, I'll check the class rooms, but all the doors are locked. She's wearing a Disney Cinderella dress with long gloves.

(TEACHER 3 *exits.*)

TEACHER 1: Thanks to Winchester we're locking inside doors.

TEACHER 2: And wrapping the chain link fence with barbed wire. Did you know that Samantha's mother caught her husband with a *very young teenager* at a beach motel?

TEACHER 1: Oh God. You're not kidding.

TEACHER 3: *(Offstage)* Samantha!

TEACHER 1: Should we look for Samantha?

TEACHER 2: I'm sure she's locked herself in the teacher's bathroom. That girl's extremely private.

TEACHER 1: A lot of the kids are not dealing well with the potty.

TEACHER 2: Samantha's doing that weird thing with her pull-ups up her crotch. Sort of lap dance for tots.

TEACHER 3: *(Offstage)* Samantha!

TEACHER 1: Samantha and the others do go at it all the time.

TEACHER 2: All the kids pick on Samantha! Because she's five years old going on thirteen.

TEACHER 1: True.

TEACHER 3: *(Offstage)* Samantha!

TEACHER 2: Her Mom's dressing her up like JonBennet Ramsey

TEACHER 1: *(Calls to her loudly)* Did you find Samantha?

TEACHER 3: *(Re-enters, holding the gloves to a Cinderella costume)* I can't find her *anywhere*!

(End of scene)

Scene Four

(DAVID WINCHESTER's prison cell. He is alone. it is
evening. a spare light bulb illuminates the tiny space.
He takes out from under his cot a very large jar. His speech
at first seems directed to the audience, but eventually veers
to the jar which contains an indistinct floating shape.)

WINCHESTER: Science was once the core of my life.
Nothing else made any sense to me.
In truth the irrational mind is supreme.
And physical logic forms a prison.
Could my luck return twofold?
Thanks to a Burmese inmate
Who sells sinful exotics
Outside the dank laundry room,
I have cultivated inside
This factory-size pickle jar
A demonic creature from Asia.
Marinating in vinegar and brine.
Killer, killer, inside a jar
(He unscrews the lid. smoke rises off the stage or from the
jar.) We see a fetus—*a toyol*
Unearthed from a foul grave
Killer, killer, sickly green
Like a bloated dill pickle
This vile creature flies
Your teeth sharper
than any shark.
With your one broad smile
An entire house is poisoned.

(Perhaps the toyol's *fetal head appears from inside the jar.)*

(End of scene)

Scene Five

(Two Chicano farm workers, RUBIO *and* DIEGO, *from Escondido region are on a lunch break in a field of Poinsettas. A raven is cawing loudly.)*

RUBIO: *(Softly)* My truck died.

DIEGO: Of course it died. I told you to sell that *truque la samana pasado, cabron.*

RUBIO: *¿Sabes que, compre una bicy?*

DIEGO: You bought a bike? Oh, *estodo carnal.*

RUBIO: My truck was like my girlfriend. And I called her *Mi Chi Chi.*

DIEGO: Forget about *su truquita.* You have too many *chi chi's*, Rubio.

RUBIO: *Ya se.* I'm so *lucky!*

DIEGO: *Sabes ques...*I see this girl in the fields.

RUBIO: Nina?

DIEGO: She glows! *Vien relusiente. No madre.* I worry about this *chavala*, Rubio.

(The audience sees CHANTELLE *in the distance haze.)*

RUBIO: Diego!

DIEGO: Who wants trouble? *Esta por todos lados,* like she's lost.

RUBIO: Lost?

DIEGO: *Si.* Red hair. In the shadows *puerdes ver sus* angel wings.

RUBIO: *Angel wings?*

DIEGO: Maybe she's the *el jefe's* kid?

RUBIO: He got no grandchildren.

DIEGO: *Aveses pienso que me llama* Diego, Diego... Diego...

CHANTELLE: Diego...Diego...Diego...

(The audience hears her, but not the workers.)

RUBIO: And why the hell does she call you?

DIEGO: Because, I play the harmonica *like a professional.*

RUBIO: Are you done with your *taco de frijoles con huevo*?

DIEGO: No. Tuna. It's shit! You want the rest?

(RUBIO grabs sandwich and continues to eat.)

DIEGO: This girl looks like Chantelle. I ask God how does this happen? Winchester suffocated her. It's so sick. *La mato.* He's going to hell and his ass will burn forever!

RUBIO: He'll die in jail. *Un pinche maton se lo va a hechar en el shower. (Slices throat with finger and gross sound. Takes bite of sandwich) ¿Que es esta mierda? ¿Aguacate y tuna?*

DIEGO: It's fucking bad tuna. *¡Hija de la chingada!* The *pinche* smell. I told you not to eat it.

(Seeing CHANTELLE)

DIEGO: That's her!

RUBIO: *¿Donde?*

DIEGO: By the trees.

CHANTELLE: Diego...Diego...Diego...

RUBIO: *Ay buey.* She's glowing.

DIEGO: We should tell the *el jefe.*

RUBIO: Simon!

DIEGO: You tell him. He likes you.

RUBIO: Bullshit.

CHANTELLE: Rubio...Rubio...Rubio...

RUBIO: *¡Dios mio! Esa nina* could be ...

DIEGO & RUBIO: Chantelle.

(CHANTELLE *disappears suddenly.*)

(*End of scene*)

Scene Six

(*A house in city heights* and *campus.* JESSIE *carries voice recorder and a notepad meets with a Somali Bantu representative,* HAMADI, *who doesn't look directly at her until later.* Conversation is anti-chronological and somewhat non-realistic, *since* JESSIE *is in two locations and two times.* HAMADI's *attention is on the series of boxes that he's unpacking. He is excited by the boxes and assumes his son is coming to San Diego.* JESSIE *starts out lecturing the audience.*)

JESSIE: (*To audience*) The Somali Bantu is a thriving new community in City Heights. Escaping Somalian warlords, approximately two thousand Bantu refugees came to San Diego between 1996 and 2000. (*Pause*) Hamadi is the Bantu leader here. He lives with three young daughters. Hamadi likes the California climate, the fresh produce, and has an unreported cable box to watch *The Sopranos.*

HAMADI: (*With joy, to* JESSIE) These packages were lost for months until U P S called. My son must be coming to join his family in America. *Cha shukuru mwenyezimugu Kwa barazake Na herizake (thank God for such a magnificent blessing).*

JESSIE: The packages have the personal effects of his son, Malik, still in Africa.

HAMADI: I have legal problems in Somalia. I can't go back to visit.

JESSIE: I was horrified. One of Hamadi's boxes had the preserved bones of his son's right hand.

HAMADI: For petty crimes, hands and feet are cut off like vegetables.

JESSIE: The Somali warlords were sending Hamadi a message. I knew things ahead of time. It scared me. *Do you miss the graves of your ancestors?*

HAMADI: We wash the dead with care, take white cloth, cover the body. *(Pause)* When somebody you love dies and there can be another life—that is good news. Our grandfathers refused the Somalis. Come *Day of Judgment*. No matter where you are. We say—*Mahakam niyaya ya mwenyezimugu tu hakuna matuhu*—Judgment is above the highest mountain.

JESSIE: America?

HAMADI: America is so strange. I want my children to stay Muslim, *with Bantu traditions.* Somalis have done many bad things, taken our farms. Killing our people. Raping Bantu women. Islam says God will punish.

JESSIE: You have a son you left in Somalia. Malik?

HAMADI: I haven't seen Malik in three years. How do you know?

JESSIE: Malik's your oldest and he was looking after your house...

HAMADI: *(Acknowledging* JESSIE's *shine)*
Was? In the name of Allah
Most benevolent, ever-merciful.
All praise be to Allah.

JESSIE: *(To audience)* I knew they killed his boy.

HAMADI: Please look at me, young woman.

(Their eyes finally meet.)

JESSIE: Yes?

HAMADI: *Tell me about my son. (Pause)* Please. I do not want lies.

JESSIE: I'm so very sorry. Your son is dead. There is evidence inside these boxes.

HAMADI: *(A* crie de coeur, *a long pause, perhaps in Swahili or Bantu)* I am going to lose my mind! *Na endelea kupoteza ubongo wangu ah mwenyezimugu ah mugu wangu. (He hits one or two boxes with his hands.)* Oh God, Oh God, Oh God of mine!

(Lights change. passage of time. We hear Somali music and HAMADI *is praying in Arabic.)*

HAMADI: *Bismi lahi rahmani al rahim*
Al hamdu lilahi rabil ala mina al rah mani al rahimi maliki yau midini iiyaka na abudu waiyaka nastaqinu ihidina siradha mustaqini siradha ladina an amta alehi qerin maqadubin alehim walili thalina amin wali asri inalin sana lafi husr ina ladina amanu wa aminu salihati watawasow bilhaq watawasobilmar hamat

JESSIE: I left Hamadi alone for the morning. I came back later that day.

HAMADI: *(Completing his pray. Music fades.)* I don't have the heart to open another box.

*(*JESSIE *nods with compassion.)*

HAMADI: How do you know these things?

JESSIE: I see shapes. I hear words. I don't know.

HAMADI: You are like the spirit of Wanankhucha. A Zigua leader from East Africa for our hard journeys. You see God's light. Wanankhucha led our people out of slavery into the Juba River valley. Say her name.

JESSIE: Wanankhucha.

HAMADI: She is like Moses helping the children of Israel cross the Red Sea. You have seen me at my worst.

JESSIE: I see how deeply you love your son.

HAMADI: *(Subdued smile)* What about *your grieving? Your father is dead.*

JESSIE: He passed away seventeen years ago.

HAMADI: Seventeen years marks a Bantu generation. Your father's memory is in your hands. His spirit counts numbers over and over. The numbers get very big. It is a form of punishment and yet he needs the numbers.

JESSIE: How do you know this, Hamadi?

HAMADI: I just know. *(Pause)* When somebody disappears, you miss the person a million times. *Have you cooled your father's bones?*

JESSIE: His bones?

HAMADI: In the hereafter, what does one really know? *You have to cool the bones of death, or these bones will haunt you. Yes?* I will show you. And you absolve the sins. You will come back tomorrow night, yes?

JESSIE: Yes.

HAMADI: Good. You will do me a favor. *I need your help.* My son was in prison. I waited a year for him. When he was released, he would not come with me. I made a great mistake. *(Pause)* Today with his personal things here—my boy calls me but I cannot hear him. *Be Wanankhucha.* It is safer for him to reach you. In a Bantu ritual. *(Pause)* There is strength around your eyes. I see the color. The spirits trust you. You have ancestry to us. When people sleep, you bring my voice to my son. So you must come to me at night. It is not Muslim practice, but Bantu beliefs years before Muslim life. You provide the link.

JESSIE: How can I possibly do that?

HAMADI: Because you came on this day to see me when his boxes came.

JESSIE: I have no magic.

HAMADI: We only need belief.

JESSIE: *(To the audience)* I doubted him. How could I be something that I'm not?

HAMADI: Danger if you ignore God—*now that you can see pure blue light.* These are my child's shirts, his books, the holy relics of his right hand. *Please, my son's bones need your help. (Stoically, he removes a bone from the box.)*

(End of scene)

Scene Seven

(On the Coronado ferry dock. Sounds of seagulls and ferry horns. JESSIE's mother holds flowers and talks to the sky. In parallel time, BENNY is also addressing the sky.)

MOM: Martin. Martin. Martin, my beloved. Happy anniversary, darling. *(Pause)* I take my clothes to an old tailor from Tijuana. His name is Benny. But that must be his nickname. He's native American. A tailor but he's more than a sewing machine. Benny heals people with plain talk and with precious garments. He lives above his store on Avenida Revolucion. I found Benny after a friend told me how magical he was. Like an El Greco painting, his fingers are incredibly long and beautiful. He looks much younger than his age. *Decades younger.* I'm very attracted to him. *(Pause)* Martin, I know you don't hear me yet I feel you nearby.

BENNY: For twenty five years I search for you, my dear wife. Where can you be?

Won't you call me by my name? Won't you hold my
hand one more time?

MOM: The thing about Benny is his hidden world.
The other side. He seems haunted. Something Jessie
could appreciate. Your single daughter—in a strict
PhD program that has only gay men and two very
vocal lesbians.

BENNY: My darling wife struck by a freakish accident in
San Diego. That much I can believe. Will I ever know?
I hope no evil took you from my heart.

MOM: He trusts me. Benny has a quiet dignity, Martin.
His wife's body hasn't been found. Benny said...

MOM/BENNY: ...evil comes and evil goes.

MOM: But I'm talking to thin air. My darling? (*Shift in
voice*) Martin?

BENNY: (*Sings his* Wife's Song *in native tongue while*
MOM *continues her text*)
She kissed me under a black cloud
And the heavy sky turned bright
The cold wind broke through so loud
Song birds and eagles fell from sight
How can you love a spirit, she asked.
In song, I said.
In song, I said.
How can you marry a spirit, she asked.
In song, I said.
In song, I said.
We dance, We cling
We sleep, We sing.

MOM: Can you see me? I still fit into this dress, your
favorite. I let out the seams just a bit. (*Pause*) It's our
wedding anniversary today. And I'm tossing flowers
into the water for you. (*Tosses flowers over the rail*) I love
you. I'm here for you. You're in my dreams. I forgive

you. Please forgive me. I was so jealous of your freedom. I hated when you traveled overseas *and brought back hellish things*. I hated your secrecy. Please hear me.

(BENNY *concludes his song and hums the melody.*)

MOM: I met a man who's very gentle. Won't you let me spend more time with him? *(Pause)* His full name is Benny Sweetwater.

BENNY: *(To* MOM*)* Hello, Phyllis.

MOM: *(Seeing* BENNY *for the first time.)* Benny?

BENNY: Yes.

MOM: What a coincidence! What are you doing here?

BENNY: I like the ferries that go to Coronado. What are you doing here?

MOM: Coming here empowers me, makes me feel brave.

BENNY: And the water calms me. You know, you look wonderful in that dress.

MOM: Yes, your handiwork.

BENNY: Thank you.

MOM: *(Fog horn)* How funny.

BENNY: Is it?

MOM: I talk to my dead husband here, Benny.

BENNY: I talk to my dead wife here, Phyllis.

MOM: What a coincidence.

BENNY: *(Fog horn)* We talk on the ferry.

(Second fog horn)

(End of scene)

Scene Eight

(JESSIE *and* FELIX *walking inside Old Town's Whaley House. She has a camera and sneaks photos of the interior spaces. We see slides of her photos.*)

FELIX: You're a brilliant lecturer.

JESSIE: Thank you.

FELIX: But why do you hold back from saying what you really believe?

JESSIE: It's essential that I maintain academic credibility. My PhD is on the line. Ghosts, U F Os, Crop Circles— fuck, my doctoral program isn't the Learning Annex.

FELIX: You have second sight, Jessie. I'll prove it. Tell me something about my secret life.

JESSIE: *(Joking)* You died over a year ago but you still can't get rid of all your jewelry.

FELIX: *(Initially shaken by her response. Mock defensive)* I didn't die, I just don't wear cologne anymore.

JESSIE: *Quel damage!* I was teasing you.

FELIX: Oh.

JESSIE: You don't like being teased? *(Pause)* Teasing is a form of affection.

FELIX: Yeah, I know. I went to boarding school. Why are we meeting at the Whaley House?

JESSIE: It's almost Halloween. Whaley's the top site on the national registry haunted mansions

FELIX: Jess.

JESSIE: Three weeks ago I saw the *ectoplasma* of a young girl in the lobby. Chantelle Van Buren. I had to come back with a special camera.

FELIX: Chantelle Van Buren?

JESSIE: The girl who was abducted a year ago.

FELIX: But the young girl who haunts the house...

JESSIE: Ran into a clothes line...

FELIX: ...and lost her head. The child's name was Violet Whaley.

JESSIE: Violet Whaley's not the girl that I saw here. Chantelle is struggling. I see her in my dreams. Whaley beckons her because it's the "Hilton for ghostly children".

(Slides of the nursery upstairs)

FELIX: You deny ghosts in your published writings. Yet you're trying to prove cold science wrong.

JESSIE: I once thought the moon was king of all ghosts and, with each full moon, all the wandering ghosts on earth would shine at night. As a child I thought I'd marry a ghost. Crazy? I was afraid of dying—until I had my first period. Then I thought I'd live forever because my periods moved to the lunar calendar and whenever I bled I could read people's minds.

FELIX: Yes, yes. I understand perfectly. Bruce Willis. "I see dead people".

JESSIE: Look, my father chased ghosts and lost his mind.

FELIX: What do you mean?

JESSIE: He stopped writing books and hunted Malaysian sorcerers. *(Pause)* In my dreams, Chantelle Van Buren seeks revenge against Winchester. The man who killed her. And that's one reason why Chantelle is caught between two worlds.

FELIX: Your dreams are scary.

JESSIE: *(Owning up to a truth)* Yeah. I've even written to Winchester at Calapatria Prison asking for an interview.

(Sound of wind. CHANTELLE *appears.* FELIX *sees her.* JESSIE *does not.)*

JESSIE: What is it?

FELIX: *(Covering his reaction to* CHANTELLE*)* Ghosts, Jess, can trick you.

JESSIE: How do you know?

FELIX: Ghosts are like distant stars that have died centuries ago—still we think they're alive because we see their glow for countless light years.

JESSIE: But a star is a billion trillion miles away...

FELIX: ...while a ghost can be tugging at your hair.

*(*JESSIE *turns toward* CHANTELLE *who saunters off.* JESSIE *cannot see her.)*

FELIX: You know, you have very luminous eyes.

JESSIE: Thank you.

FELIX: One eye is brown, the other eye hazel. One eye sees *the present,* the other eye sees everything *but the present. (Holds her gently)* So, what do you think?

JESSIE: *(Sweetly)* About what?

FELIX: Do you think I'm too good looking for my height?

(He kisses her hard on the mouth.)

JESSIE: You just kissed me.

FELIX: *(Feeling a faux pas)* I thought you were expecting it. Your lips were glistening.

JESSIE: Glistening?

FELIX: I'm sorry... Tell me your best ghost story.

JESSIE: Thirty four years ago, my Dad chased an Asian demon right back into a jar.

FELIX: Cool.

JESSIE: Now you.

FELIX: August 2003, at Christus Saint Joseph Hospital in Houston, Doctor Hitoshi Nikaidoh lost his head in an elevator. The doors trapped him and Nikaidon's neck was sheared as the elevator rose. His body was found in the shaft along with two pagers.

JESSIE: Oh, Christ!

FELIX: And his assistant, Karin Steinau, was with him.

JESSIE: Stop!

FELIX: Steinau was stuck for an hour with Hitoshi's severed head until the rescue team came.

(JESSIE *wraps her hands over his mouth.*)

JESSIE: *Please stop!*

FELIX: The maintenance company got reamed up the kazoo.

JESSIE: How do you hear about these God-awful stories?

FELIX: They're in our union newsletter. That's right. I'm a union guy.

JESSIE: Why do you like me, Felix?

(CHANTELLE *appears with rope and watches.*)

FELIX: Because I think you're gorgeous. (*He kisses her again.*) Are you happy, Jessie?

JESSIE: Yes.

FELIX: (CHANTELLE *gently tugs* FELIX *behind his trouser belt.*) Then why would you want to sleep with a ghost?

(*End of scene*)

Scene Nine

(WINCHESTER alone in his cell picks up a bundle of letters and scatters them in one gesture.)

WINCHESTER: Look at this crap! Fifteen, twenty letters? Do I look like a pathetic, moronic pen-pal? What must I do with this ivory tower nut? The arrogant stupid twat. This—"Jessie Gordon?"—writes daily asking for an interview. "Ms Gordon" is a scholar *and* a journalist *a la* Truman Capote. But she's got to be a blind bitch. I do not give interviews. I do not sign autographs. I don't kiss softly on the cheek. Her last letter mentioned my redemption and revelation. What is she, fucking Mother Teresa? *(Pause)* If I get one more letter, she'll get *something lovely* from me, *my pet. She'll get you!*

(End of scene)

Scene Ten

(JESSIE, approaches the podium, a few minutes before her lecture. She is startled to see CHANTELLE on the floor by the podium. JESSIE drops her lecture notes.)

CHANTELLE: *(Sings)*
Hush, little baby, don't say a word
Mama's gonna buy you a mockin'bird

If that mockin' bird don't sing
Mama's gonna buy you a diamond ring

If that diamond ring turns brass,
Mama's gonna buy you a looking glass

If that looking glass gets broke
Mama's gonna buy you a billy goat

(Helping JESSIE collect her papers)

Hush darling Jessie, find Samantha.
She's not in a cage, sweet little panther
But she's not me, she's not you
Please set us free, pick up the clue.

(Lights shift. CHANTELLE *vanishes.)*

(End of scene)

Scene Eleven

*(*JESSIE *puts her laptop on the podium. When she raises the cover we hear students in the lecture hall. She then lectures while we see several slides of brilliant, colorful hummingbirds and butterflies. She will see in the lecture hall her father— half dressed in a tattered tuxedo.)*

JESSIE: A century ago, anthropology served as the absurd wall between physical science and cultural awareness. Clearly, each study borrowed the work of the other in an attempt to find the rare missing link. Indifferent to anthropology, the native peoples of Latin America. Like their ancestors believe that spirits would return as hummingbirds and butterflies. Linking the human spirit with...

(Reaches out her hand, a butterfly lands on her finger.)

DAD: A gentle, fleeting butterfly.

JESSIE: Dad?

DAD: One, one, two, three, five, eight...

JESSIE: Oh my God! *(Quietly stunned)* Oh my God! Daddy?

(He continues to count)

DAD: ...eight, thirteen, twenty-one, thirty-four, fifty-five, eighty-nine.

JESSIE: I'm in the middle of a lecture!

(He smiles, but doesn't look directly at her.)

JESSIE: I'm not dreaming. I'm not dreaming. Why, after all these years?

(He continues)

DAD: One hundred forty-four, two hundred thirty-three, three hundred seventy-seven, six hundred ten.

JESSIE: Daddy, talk to me, damn it! What's that smell?

(He spray Binaca into his mouth.)

JESSIE: Damn it, what are you doing?

DAD: I'm getting dressed.

JESSIE: *I'm in the middle of a lecture!*

DAD: Everyone's left.

JESSIE: I haven't seen you for ages.

DAD: Darling, that's why I changed my clothes.

JESSIE: Last time I saw your shadow was fifteen years ago.

DAD: When you lost your virginity?

JESSIE: That's none of your business, Martin.

DAD: I'm *still* your father.

JESSIE: Where did my students go?

DAD: To their next class. *You've been staring at me for over ten minutes, Jessie.*

JESSIE: Oh God!

DAD: *(Almost whispering)* Shhhhhh, not so loud. I'm counting softly. Nine hundred eighty-seven, one thousand five hundred ninety-seven...

JESSIE: Are you *still* wearing these awful wing tips?

DAD: Two thousand five hundred eighty-four...
four thousand one hundred eighty-one...

JESSIE: Stop counting!

DAD: I can't stop. Otherwise I'll fall. Counting is my
handrail. Ingenious. The Fibonacci sequence. Four
thousand one hundred eighty-one... Code of the Golden
Mean and the exact growth pattern of all spiraling
leaves. I waited so long for you to find me.

JESSIE: Find you? I didn't find you.

DAD: Then how the hell am I here?

JESSIE: I don't understand.

DAD: *The shine.* Runs in my side of the family. Five
thousand seven hundred seventy-eight, five thousand
seven hundred sixty-six...is that the Jewish New Year?
Oh shit, I'm stuck.

JESSIE: Why now? Why can I see you now?

DAD: You've always had the shine, Jessie, but you fight
it.Please help me with my tie. Nine thousand nine
hundred fifty-nine.

(Sensing JESSIE's *reaction, he tries to be amusing.)*

DAD: You're coming into a brilliant perception of good
and evil. And I want you to stay alive.

JESSIE: Daddy!

DAD: You'll see a pattern. A demon is over our house.
To fight it, be free of all fears. To survive, be absolutely
indifferent to death. Fifteen thousand seven hundred
thirty-seven. *(Pause)* You're much stronger than me.
Jacket please. You got to help me, Jessie. *(Affected
voice—some Hollywood actor)* "No reputable hotel will
give me a goddamn room!"

JESSIE: Did you kill yourself?

DAD: I made a terrible mistake. I paid for that mistake.

JESSIE: Don't apologize for Ted.

DAD: I knew my brother was fighting some moral sickness.

JESSIE: He was more than a goddamn sick victim! Uncle was twisted.

DAD: Honey, I was fighting for my life in Malaysia. I killed a sorcerer and his minions struck back through my brother. Can't talk about it anymore, Jessie. Oh Christ, I lost count. One, one, two, three, five, eight, thirteen, twenty-one, thirty-four... *(Sound of a "cosmic" pager. Starts to exit)* They're calling for me. How do I look?

JESSIE: Wait, Daddy. Turn this way!

(He does. She produces a small camera)

JESSIE: Smile. Come on.

(A flash goes off. He shields his eyes.)

JESSIE: Is that so hard?

DAD: Yes.

(End of scene)

Scene Twelve

(BENNY and JESSIE are in his Tijuana tailor shop. There is a chatty macaw perched on a bird stand. BENNY is working a heavy steam iron on his wife's dress.)

JESSIE: I thought you'd be a *much older* man.

BENNY: I am *an older man.* *(Smiling warmly)* But with two hands I can lift a small car. You like crossing the border?

JESSIE: Love Tijuana. Hate the Border.

JESSIE/BENNY: Long lines.

BENNY: You know, I like your mother very much.

JESSIE: Thank you. She said you were nearly sixty five but you look half that age.

BENNY: She has love for life and has been very good to me. But your mother worries about you all the time. *(Pause)* What is that?

JESSIE: A miniature recorder. *(She flips out an audio cassette from the recorder.)*

BENNY: Please don't. Put it away.

(She's slow to react and he mashes the cassette with his steam iron.)

BENNY: I'm very sorry.

JESSIE: *(With some irony)* May I take notes at least?

BENNY: Ask Benny anything.

JESSIE: Thank you.

BENNY: Many people wish the living and the dead would stay far apart.

JESSIE: I think that's very true.

BENNY: *(Glances at the forms under JESSIE's hand)* Do you believe in ghosts?

JESSIE: That is one of my questions to ask you.

BENNY: Maybe the question is upside down.

JESSIE: What do you mean?

BENNY: Maybe you need to ask—*Do ghosts believe in you?*

JESSIE: How can I ask that?

BENNY: Just ask yourself. *(Smiles)* I can make rags into perfect clothes. And rich people might as well wear

rags. *(Signals an antique gold gown hanging above)*
This was my wife's favorite dress.

JESSIE: It's beautiful.

BENNY: You are very close to her size, but she had no
neck. Even a turtle has a neck.

*(He sings a stanza of his wife's song and is interrupted by the
bird.)*

MACAW: *¡La mamacita es bonita!*

BENNY: Here is my favorite color thread. *(Hands her the
golden thread)*

JESSIE: Very chatty bird.

BENNY:	MACAW:
Shaddup!	"Big hips launch ships!"
(To bird)	

BENNY: I want you to help me find my wife's grave site.

JESSIE: *How* can I help you?

BENNY: I know what you can do, young lady. *(Pause)*
My wife had epilepsy. I just know she's dead.
Disappeared during a storm along the waterfront.
1979. On the other side of the border. San Diego
authorities have no idea where her body is. I went
to every morgue and cemetery. I wrote letters to the
mayor and the Indian tribes. Nothing. Silence. Dead air.
So I left San Diego.

JESSIE: I'm so sorry for you.

BENNY: In America, God is a casino. Filthy quarters
and nickels fall from the sky. *(Pause)* Generations ago
women in my family wore a willow bark skirt. That has
more meaning to me. *(Pause)* I know a little about your
father's passing. When a family member in my tribe
dies, we cut all the family hair short. Very few of us left.
My wife loved to ride the Coronado ferry. And now I

ride the ferry with your mother. This is a family
bracelet.

(Presents it to JESSIE*)*

BENNY: I give it to you. Please. It might spare you from
evil spirits.

(We now hear BENNY*'s wife voice singing the song.)*

BENNY: We need only a day this week to find my wife.
You have a magic eye, Jessie. I can feel it. Please. Help a
very lonely man.

(End of scene)

Scene Thirteen

*(*JESSIE *records notes into her tape recorder as she reviews
projected slides of* BENNY *and* HAMADI *in her campus office.)*

JESSIE: October 26, 2005. Two recent interviews asked
me to intervene in their personal affairs beyond the
grave. The same two interviews touched on my father's
death. Very strange. *(Pause)* I visited the Islamic
cemetery nearby. Muslims must say—*Salem Aley
Khon*—May peace be upon you. I am drawn to all
graveyards. In Egypt, graves look like clay huts. Here,
Islamic graves are grassy areas with plaques and simple
stones. Muslims say *Duaa* which asks God to forgive
the deceased. I pray that Samantha is not dead.

*(*FELIX *enters quietly with pizza.)*

JESSIE: My father was Christian yet he was intrigued
by Islam's angels. He called them *Jinns*. But *Jinns*, for
Muslims, are somewhere between angels and humans.

FELIX: *(Indian or Persian accent)* I could be a *Jinn*.

JESSIE: Is that right?

FELIX: I like the sound of the word—*Jinns*.
I like the sharp smell of—*Jesus*.
I like the mystical *Jews*.

JESSIE: And I like sweet *ju-ju bees*! *(Pause)* I could be a *Jinn*.

JESSIE/FELIX: *Jinn... Jinn... Jinn...*

(They laugh. She takes a quick photo of FELIX*)*

FELIX: Hope you're hungry. Box is still hot.

JESSIE: *(A projection of a very blurry* FELIX *photo)* How is it that all the photos I take of you are all fucked up?

FELIX: Like Sean Penn, I'm not camera friendly. *(Playfully takes her microphone and intones)* October 12, 2005. Alain Jourden, a French fisherman, held on to his championship title. Master snail spitter. Able to propel a snail thirty-one feet! Jourden, age forty-three, beat back a hundred and ten rivals from fourteen countries!

JESSIE: You're fucking crazy, Felix. *(Laughing)*

FELIX: This is what makes France a great nation.

JESSIE: Well, I think you're great. And you can return the compliment.

FELIX: I want to sleep with you. Whooops. Who the hell said that? *(Opens pizza box)*

JESSIE: Don't rush this, Felix.

FELIX: How old were you when you first saw a ghost?

JESSIE: Four. *(She has a passing abdominal cramp.)*

FELIX: Are you sick?

JESSIE: Just cramps. Shit. Want to go on a drive today?

FELIX: Where to?

JESSIE: Dehesa Road. To talk to the people on the Samantha Shepard's search party. (*She advances slides to set of photos of missing girls in the county.*)

FELIX: (*Reads names of the tagged photos*) JonBenet Ramsey, Chatelle Van Buren, Samantha Shepard... missing girls aren't part of your dissertation. Were you molested as a child?

JESSIE: What?

FELIX: I thought you trusted me.

JESSIE: Did you know that Laura Bush killed her school boyfriend?

FELIX: That's not what I asked.

JESSIE: She drove *her sedan* through a stop sign and smashed *his jeep*. 1963. They were both seventeen. She had to have been drinking. What are the odds of that happening?

FELIX: Who gives a fuck? What happened to *you*?

JESSIE: You're a pest, Felix. It's not a fairy tale. (*Pause*) My Mom was in L.A. for the weekend and my uncle was visiting. Without warning Dad hopped a plane and left me with his brother. So Uncle Teddy drove me to Cuyamaca State Park. I was four. He spilled a can of coke on my lap. He took everything off—my dress, underwear, and was very clumsy with a dish towel. I slapped his hands away, but he began to tickle me so hard that I peed. And then he undid his pants. So I picked up a dead branch and swatted him on his Davy Crockett. That's when I saw a ghost come out of the woods. Very tall. Pale as the moon. And the thing knocked out my uncle cold.

FELIX: Did you tell your folks?

(*She shakes her head "yes" delicately.*)

JESSIE: No one knew what to do. I never saw my uncle
again and the bastard died of lung cancer.
So a ghost saved a little girl.

FELIX: But can a girl save a ghost?

(End of scene)

Scene Fourteen

(WINCHESTER's cell)

WINCHESTER: Money flies out of my stubby hands.
I had to bribe five prison guards
With half of my life's savings!
They were about to take you away
My darling precious.
They laugh at me.
Think it's all a joke.
Just a jar of thick sudsy water.
When a prison door is ajar,
This jar unlocks any door.
Gertrude Stein said it best:
A jar is a jar is a jar

(End of scene)

Scene Fifteen

*(Talking with the farm workers from the workers' earlier
scene, same location. JESSIE is in mid-interview.)*

JESSIE: I'm glad that your daughter arranged for us
to meet today. I heard about what happened from
Soledad. She's in my class at school. I want to help you.
Have you talked with anyone else?

RUBIO: No.

DIEGO: Just our wives.

RUBIO: *Eso no es lo que quiere decir, Diego.*

DIEGO: I know what she meant. You don't like my wife, *carbon*!

JESSIE: What else did you see?

RUBIO: *Vino la policia.*

JESSIE: Did the cops see you?

RUBIO & DIEGO: No, no!!

RUBIO	DIEGO:
Pos quien nos va a ver	No one sees us!
Ni nos hablan	No one talks to us!

JESSIE: How old was the girl?

RUBIO: Six or seven.

JESSIE: Mexican?

DIEGO: No.

RUBIO: *Y su pelo, bien roja.*

DIEGO: She has red hair. Her hair glows like lamp on fire.

JESSIE: And you believe she was the Van Buren girl from Del Mar?

DIEGO: Not every part of her died.

RUBIO: *¡Hombre!*

DIEGO: It happens, you see, when you are killed—before your time.

RUBIO: *Tu espiritu.*

DIEGO: Your spirit fights for revenge. Sometimes *un angelito* can help you.
She was left to the vultures in the desert.

RUBIO: *Y sin ropa.*

DIEGO: Naked. Disgusting.

JESSIE: But the girl you saw had clothes on?

DIEGO: A ghost can borrow clothes.

RUBIO: *Es facil.*

DIEGO: A ghost can fool you.

(CHANTELLE *emerges but they don't see her.*)

CHANTELLE: I see the moon and the moon sees me.

JESSIE: *(She doesn't see* CHANTELLE, *but hears her.)* I see. Why are you talking with me?

DIEGO: We don't want to be cursed.

JESSIE: You think I can stop a curse?

RUBIO: Simon.

JESSIE: Why do you believe such a thing?

DIEGO: *Mi hija.*

RUBIO: His daughter says good things about you. *Va a ser una doctora.*

DIEGO: Soledad says you have some magic.

RUBIO: *Yo pienso que si.* One of your eyes is brown.

DIEGO: The other is blue.

RUBIO: *Andele, desenbruje nos por favor.*

DIEGO: Stop the curse away before it comes, please.

JESSIE: *(She hands them a disposible camera.)* Here. Keep the camera in case you see this little girl again. And this is my card.

RUBIO: *¿Entonces nos va a ayudar?*

JESSIE: Yes. I'll do whatever you need if you will help me find the little girl.

(Lights change. We lose farm workers. JESSIE *sees* CHANTELLE *in the distance and* CHANTELLE *acknowledges* JESSIE.*)*

JESSIE: Chantelle?

CHANTELLE: *(Singing)* I see the moon
And the moon sees me
The moon sees the somebody I'd like to see.
God bless the moon and God bless me
God bless the somebody I'd like to see!

JESSIE: Chantelle. Where is Samatha? Is she alive?

CHANTELLE: *(Singing)*
Samantha comes
Samantha goes.
The old man drums
A jar with his toes.

(End of scene)

Scene Sixteen

(Wanankhucha ritual. Moonlight. Outdoors. Smoke in the air. African drumming. HAMADI *enters dressed in wrapped pants and a ceremonial Bantu colored robe with arms bare and turban. He brings a zebra tail whisk, an iron bell, rattle made of calabash gourd, ankle and wrist bracelet made of bells, rattles, shells.)*

HAMADI: *(Laying a white mat before the altar, he repeats the invocation) Taharah. Al-Wudu Bismilla-Hir-Rahma-Nir-Rah'im (In the name of Allah, the Beneficent, the Merciful)*

*(*JESSIE *enters, barefoot, dressed in ceremonial Bantu costume with a black veil covering her face.* HAMADI *dabs white mud on his face.)*

HAMADI: You are Wanankhucha tonight.
Ash-Hadu All ilaha illallahu wa-ash-hadu an-na
muhammadan 'abduhu-wa rasuluh
(I am testifying that there is no God but God)
To cool the bones, you have to cleanse your heart.
Now you have to whisper softly.

(JESSIE begins to whisper, repeating what HAMADI says to her.)

HAMADI: To cool the bones, you have to give purity.

(HAMADI waves the vase with incense in front of JESSIE's nose.)

HAMADI: We fill your breath with pure wind.
A blindfold covers your eyes.
Now you have to walk quietly
Inside a three pointed circle.

(JESSIE begins to walk as a blind person.)

HAMADI: To cool the bones, you have to sing praise.

(JESSIE might sing something softly in Bantu.)

HAMADI: The blindfold comes off.

(Removes the veil from JESSIE's face)

HAMADI: We adorn your face with the powder of sandalwood.

(Adorns her face with Sandalwood powder)

HAMADI: We pour the petals of roses over your eyes.

(Rubs JESSIE's face with rose petals)

HAMADI: Bones are the last remains. *(Tosses one of his son's bones on the ground)* Found in God's comforting earth. *(Tosses another bone)* A circle is a triangle is a circle *(Tosses another bone)* A mystical circle has four great doors.

(Tosses another bone and places JESSIE in center of bones)

HAMADI: Three doors are exotic.
The fourth door is evil.
You have to open each door.

(*Places the rattle bracelets on* JESSIE's *left arm and left ankle. Music becomes more aggressive.* JESSIE's *singing becomes incoherent. she begins to rave.* HAMADI *coaxes her into a ceremonial dance, which may mimic ordinary house chores such as measuring, pounding rice, washing dishes, stirring the fire, drawing well water and carrying it home.*)

HAMADI: (*Crying out in Swahili*) Taireni!

JESSIE: (*Loud in response*) Taiti, tai!

(JESSIE *and* HAMADI *repeat their call and response.* HAMADI *rings a small iron bell seven times. As* JESSIE *dances more feverishly her mouth begins to foam.*)

HAMADI: (*Perhaps repeating in Bantu*) Wanankhucha, you are honored with praise. Send me the voice of Malik. (*Wananchucka Ni weye mwenye hishima za sifa nitumira miye sauti ya Malik*)

(*The dance becomes intense. He places a crown made of basil clusters wrapped in leaves on top of* JESSIE's *head. As dance reaches a climax he repeats.*) Lo, Io, Io, Io... (*Hey, hey, hey, hey...*) Touombe Monggou (*We pray to God*)

(JESSIE *suddenly freezes, silence.*)

JESSIE: (*As* HAMADI's *son's voice*)
It is your sweet voice I now hear, my father.
(*Ni sauit yako yedhi Neva haluse Tate*)
Life is eternal, embraced by God's grace.
(*Maisha nimilele kwakumwinkha mwenyezimigu uwedhi*)

HAMADI: Salamu aleikum (*Greetings to you*). It is your sweet voice I now hear, my son.

JESSIE: (*As* HAMADI's *son's voice*)
Life is eternal, embraced by God's grace.
(*Maisha nimilele kwakumwinkha mwenyezimigu uwedhi*)

HAMADI: Yes. Life is eternal, embraced by God's grace.

JESSIE: (*As* HAMADI's *son's voice*) A triangle is a circle is a triangle. (*Pembe tatu nizunguluko wa pembe tatu*) I feel no pain. (*Sikuwona kulumwa*)

HAMADI: Tell me again...you feel no pain.

JESSIE: (*As* HAMADI's *son's voice*) I feel no pain, Papa. (*Sikuwona kulumwa Tate*)

HAMADI: Tell me again...you can laugh.

JESSIE: (*As* HAMADI's *son's voice*) I can laugh, Papa. (*Nadhaha nikaseka Tate*)

HAMADI: Tell me again... you live and breathe.

(JESSIE *opens her mouth, but cannot speak. Perhaps her mouth is moving but we hear no sound*)

HAMADI: Embraced by God's grace, your sweet voice I now hear forever, my cherished son.

(JESSIE *collapses in* HAMADI's *arms.*)

HAMADI: A'u-thu-bil-la-hi minashaitanir rajeem (*I seek refuge in Allah from the rejected Satan*)

(*He lifts her and gently carries her away.*)

(*End of scene*)

Scene Seventeen

(*A day care center yard In Clairemont, San Diego. Two teachers are under A canopy or umbrellas.*)

TEACHER 2: Wow. Look at those heavy black clouds!

TEACHER 1: Going to rain hard on Samantha's party. All these games have to come inside.
Did you hear about the wild stuff at Poway and Mission Bay Pre-school?

TEACHER 2: No.

TEACHER 1: Last week *all the kids* were tested for *autism*.

TEACHER 2: What!

TEACHER 1: *It's like a contagion.* Seven toddlers just stopped responded to language. They just stare into space.

TEACHER 2: You're kidding?

TEACHER 1: Uh uh! The County Health Department is vaccinating the kids, but you can't inoculate against autism. It's just the government trying to avoid a law suit.

TEACHER 2: Christ, I had my daughter vaccinated.

TEACHER 1: Has her vocabulary diminished?

TEACHER 2: A little bit. Down to seventy-five words. And she'll be seven next month. Just kidding.

(TEACHER 3 *enters and we hear the percussion of a biblical hail storm.)*

TEACHER 3: Get all the children! The kids are getting pummeled! This hail storm's dropping golf balls!

TEACHER 2: Holy shit!

TEACHER 3: Where's Samantha?

TEACHER 1: She's not with us.

TEACHER 3: I sent her out to you fifteen minutes ago!

TEACHER 2: Are you sure?

TEACHER 3: Where the hell is she?

(*Sound of* SAMANTHA *crying. Sound of toyol* and peculiar light) Oh my God!

(*End of scene*)

Scene Eighteen

(WINCHESTER *in prison talks to an unseen creature in his solitary cell. He pricks his finger with a needle and drops blood into a small dish. He will feed the dish to the* toyol. *on the prison intercom, a* GUARD'S VOICE *addresses* WINCHESTER.)

GUARD'S VOICE: Winchester...lights out in five minutes!

WINCHESTER: My pet, I don't sleep well lately. I read a lot of non-fiction. Words have many double meanings. Penal code. Penetration. Possession. I see her from time to time. But Chantelle's so much different now. Shoeless and younger. And I have aged terribly. Nabokov collected butterflies, but his reputation rests with *Lolita.* (*Responding to an inaudible reply from the* toyol) No. No. No. I am in control of my emotions. I shouldn't be dreaming of catechism. I almost became a priest. I have no hole in my heart, but why do I keep bleeding? If I'm visibly angry, then God wins. Yet God created me. And I should be resolutely dead.

(*The missing pre-school girl from Scene One appears on just as a strong colored light falls in front of him.*)

WINCHESTER: (*Talks to the light*) You brought me a gift today?

SAMANTHA: I don't like bedtime. I wet my bed.

WINCHESTER: Dear Jesus...she's beautiful.

SAMANTHA: I ran away from school.

WINCHESTER: Do you know how you got here?

(*She points to the light, bells are heard.*)

WINCHESTER: How old are you?

SAMANTHA: Five. *How old are you?*

WINCHESTER: Fifty-nine. Does your mother know you are here?

SAMANTHA: No. She's with her fat boyfriend. It's my birthday.

WINCHESTER: Today?

SAMANTHA: Yes. Sing the song.

WINCHESTER: I can't sing.

SAMANTHA: Pleeeeeeeeeeeeeeeeeeeeeeeeeeeeeeeeeeease!

WINCHESTER: *(Relents and sings)*
Happy birthday to you
Happy birthday to you
Happy birthday to... ?

SAMANTHA: Samantha...

WINCHESTER: Samantha...
Happy birthday to you!

SAMANTHA: I like birds.

WINCHESTER: So do I.

SAMANTHA: What kind of birds?

WINCHESTER: Parakeets, finches, cockatiels. When my daughter was your age, I built an aviary in my backyard for her.

SAMANTHA: A girl in my school picks on me all the time.

WINCHESTER: Which girl?

SAMANTHA: She's five and one half and I hate her goddamn guts.

WINCHESTER: Do you?

SAMANTHA: You bet. I hit her with a rock. Now she's dead.

(She taps the glass. The toyol *taps back.)*

SAMANTHA: It was a really big rock. Where's Chantelle? Can you hear her?

WINCHESTER: No.

SAMANTHA: You did it to her. Chantelle is looking for Heaven. But she wants to give you something *really really bad*. *(Devilish smile)* My teacher is looking for me.

WINCHESTER: We don't have to worry about your teacher. You're quite safe with me.

(End of scene)

Scene Nineteen

(JESSIE outside a Christian bookstore on El Cajon Boulevard. QUEE, a young clerk, is washing off spray paint grafitti along the storefront window. the grafitti says "Jesus loves Mel Gibson!" They are in the middle of a conversation.)

QUEE: Man, I hate when they tag this window!

JESSIE: They just sprayed it?

QUEE: Like five minutes ago. Where are the fucking cops?

JESSIE: My friend Germaine said I had to meet you. She said your Dad was a very special person.

QUEE: *(Turning and getting a better look at JESSIE)* You're kind of cute. *(Laughs to herself)* My dad was a monk who then became a Kruu—a Shaman. He mediated between the two spheres. Not like an African medicine man. He had a Buddha shrine, with banana leaves around a lit candle. Really cool to see.

(FELIX appears, a surprise to JESSIE.)

JESSIE: What are you doing here?

FELIX: Your car's across the street.

QUEE: Romeo's following you all the way to City Heights.

FELIX: I'll buy you lunch after your interview.

QUEE: Weird statues of Thervada buddhas, bowl of dead people's hair, braided up nice with a turtle shell on top.

FELIX: All right. *You can buy me lunch.*

QUEE: *Beat it, dude! This chick is too slick for your mama.*

JESSIE: I'll meet you later, Felix!

(FELIX *leaves.*)

QUEE: That guy is a mid-wife. You know, *a doula.*

JESSIE: What makes you say that?

QUEE: Look at his hands, girl! *Doula, doula, doula*! Guy's got no shadow. *(Abrupt shift, perhaps entering shop)* So my dad was tatted up from head to toe with dragons, ancient warriors, arms, neck, ankles, his ass and penis too.

JESSIE: Yes?

QUEE: Yeah, he went too far, but—hell—that's my Daddy! Dad said the inscriptions make his skin resilient to any puncture during Khmer Rouge war. The trick worked. He was more fuckin' rubbery than the Michelin Man. *(Pause)* I was born in San Diego.

JESSIE: Why did you say my friend has no shadow?

QUEE: You must really like him. Are you afraid of death?

JESSIE: Yes.

QUEE: Hell, I'm more afraid of possession. You're making me see my father like he never died.
I feel his breath on my cheek. That never happens.

(Pause) I'm just kidding you! And maybe I'm not.
(Laughs) I'll tell you a true story. An exorcism. 1994. Yes?

JESSIE: *(Weary)* Please.

QUEE: My friend, and twenty of his best buddies were
at a Christmas party. Two girls, a Vietnamese and a
Filipina, started to act weird.

*(From a reverse angle on the store front mirror, we see
heavily wigged silhouettes of the aforementioned two girls)*

QUEE: They were possessed by *an Evil*. See.

(She points. They gyrate.)

QUEE: Their killing eyes—serious, chilling. Bodies stiff
and cold like marble. No shit. They walk like zombies.
Cousin Manny calls. Dad says "Hey, bring them over!"
It's midnight. As they walk in with the girls, our dogs
howls like the devil and his butler were here. My dad,
in a sarong, lights the candles. The Filipina girl looks
at me. I feel she's eating up my brain with forks and
knives. She's on her knees, moaning like Linda Blair,
with bony hands clinging to the Vietnamese girl.

(One of the silhoutte figures kneels and moans.)

QUEE: Cousin Manny says—"Let's get the fuck out of
here, you girl scouts!" *(Pause)* Dead silence. Dad gets a
bowl of holy water, puts the candle over a silver bowl,
chants, sits on the floor Indian-style. Says to bring the
Vietnamese girl! *(Pause)* He whispers "It's the work of
a *toyol*, separate the girls or we'll all be fucked!" Then
he sips holy water and spews it on her. Jessie!

(Water sprays at the silhoutte)

QUEE: She falls back and faints.

JESSIE: And the Filipina girl?

QUEE: She drops too. Both girls are out for minutes.
A great stink fills the room. The walls become still and

you could see powder blue. "Pi Hong"—says Dad smiling.

JESSIE: *Pi Hong?*

QUEE: Some girl's name he likes. *The chicks wake up and are like sweet little lambs!*

(We hear teenage girls braying like baby lambs.)

QUEE: Your father was not a *shaman,* but he had cool gifts.

JESSIE: My father was a college professor. Anthropology.

QUEE: For real?

JESSIE: He traveled a lot to Asia.

QUEE: It was a cover.

JESSIE: What?

QUEE: For his *secret work.* We've something in common. Our dads kept shit from us but they gave us great spirit. We both have their *birthmarks.*

(Touches her forehead and JESSIE's *head)*

QUEE: You know, there's the eternal *Ahp* A female spirit who only becomes human if she's loved with a very long tongue.

JESSIE: Interesting... *(Pause)* My dad did work in Malaysia on *mandalas* and *toyols.*

QUEE: *Toyols?* No shit? That's serious.

*(*QUEE *pulls an invisible thread from* JESSIE's *abdomen.)*

QUEE: A *toyol* is a still-born fetus dug up from its grave by a shit-face sorcerer in the dead hours.

(A startling beam of light strikes the window. JESSIE *sees the light, but* QUEE *does not.)*

QUEE: And the sorcerer brings the fetus back to life...with ungodly chants and the blood of a rooster.

(She kneels, makes a bone-chilling rooster sound) The fetus, like an evil genie, is contained inside a large jar. You feed them blood at midnight. If the owner fails, *death will be very painful.* Many Asians know the power of the *toyol.* Although I have yet to see a *Toyols-R-Us* store in Linda Vista. See, I'm G-2. I kiss both cultures and the *connecting door.*

(Red light bathes JESSIE. QUEE *now senses some danger for* JESSIE.)

QUEE: I'm actually more Christian now. Don't want to be a dead monk like dad. *(Pause)* You want a baby. That takes guts. We're born with a special number of eggs, Jessie. That's Bio 101. You know your number? You might be at the *final height.*

JESSIE: *Final height?*

QUEE: *That* would explain all the strange crap you see and the pain in your eyes.

JESSIE: *(Abdominal pain)* Oh God...

QUEE: *(An arm around* JESSIE*)* Tomorrow, let me be with you. A *toyol* has marked your womb and you got to have a powerful shield.

(End of scene)

Scene Twenty

*(*WINCHESTER, *in a painter's smock, sits inside his cell and paints something on a small easel. It might be an image from Balthus or some non-provocative image. On the other side of the stage is* FELIX. FELIX *is putting on make-up sitting or standing in front of a mirror. The monologues might dovetail into one another, or overlap in some fashion.)*

WINCHESTER:
Soon the children of this city will repeat *le petit mal.*

I see the signs of nature's love and capriciousness.
The man-eating tigers at the zoo are ill tempered.
Stray cats piss on trams and strollers *indiscriminately*.

FELIX: My skin is flaking. I have just a few days left
before I wilt into nothing.
I'm the tarot card's hanging man, all my lucky pennies
have fallen away.
I need her so much. Jessie must know. I have one more
chance at life and death.
I can give her so many things. I love Jessie Gordon!

WINCHESTER: Children stop hearing their parents.
These children are truant, ornery.
They wet their beds before midnight.
And look for the Pied Piper.
She could be the pretty Piper.
She craves the role.
Before the *gran mal*.
But I'm the real thing.

FELIX: Please God, give me this final chance. Her
mother. *Su madre. (Pause)* Her father. *Su padre. (Pause)*
Her imaginary child. *Su nina in el futuro. (Pause)*
Y yo. Su esposo.

FELIX/WINCHESTER: I am her truest man.

WINCHESTER: *(Singing)* I'm the piped piper...follow me
I'm the piped piper...follow me

(End of scene)

Scene Twenty-one

*(JESSIE and FELIX at IHOP. Signs announce daily specials
and grand opening)*

FELIX: Why are we seeing your mother? I'm not making
you meet *my mother*.

JESSIE: She's not a komodo dragon. I see her.

(She waves to her mother.)

JESSIE: Over here, Mom!

FELIX: *(Looking in the wrong direction)* She looks so young, Jessie.

JESSIE: That's not her. Over there.

MOM: Hello darling. Sorry to be late. My car stalled inside a car wash. You must be Fritz. I'm Mrs Gordon. I asked Benny to join us.

JESSIE: Benny?

MOM: The tailor from Tijuana.

(Turning to FELIX*)*

MOM: So, I understand you're an *elevator scholar*?

FELIX: Yes.

MOM: You're younger than Jessie.

FELIX: I don't hold that against her.

JESSIE: Mother!

MOM: My daughter chases ghosts.

FELIX: It's better than chasing men.

JESSIE: *(Her cell phone rings. She sees number)* Oh crap, it's my dissertation advisor. Please, Mom, don't humiliate me until I come back to the table.

(She pinches FELIX*'s arm and exits the table.)*

MOM: Do you like my Jessie?

FELIX: I'm in love your daughter.

***

JESSIE: *(Concurrent with* FELIX/MOM *dialogue above—*JESSIE *is on cell and* DAD *eavesdrops on the* *conversation) I gave the committee the last five chapters. Yes. I'll make hard copies too.*

(JESSIE *is accosted by* DAD)

DAD: Who's the new boyfriend?

JESSIE: *(Flip)* Oscar de la Hoya.

DAD: Why do you like him?

JESSIE: He's smart, cute, I can train him.

DAD: Puppy needs a good home?

JESSIE: I might even love this puppy. *(Back on cell phone, to phone conversant) Some of my interviews are in long hand. (She's making notes on a pad.)*

DAD: *(Charming, rather than ominous)* He has one foot in a grave. You do know that?

***

JESSIE: *(The following is phone chatter during* MOM's *scene.) I realize, Professor.*

***

MOM: Are you honest?

FELIX: Of course. My Dad's half Irish. The top half.

MOM: And the bottom half?

FELIX: Jewish?

MOM: Are you afraid of marriage?

JESSIE: *I have almost everything on audio too.*

FELIX: Why do Jewish men break glass?

MOM: Why do Irish men break wind?

(BENNY *joins them at the table.)*

BENNY: To make room at a crowded bar. *(Pause)* Hello, Phyllis.

MOM: Hello, Benny. How are you today?

BENNY: I'm hungry.

(He smiles at FELIX.)

***

JESSIE: *(On phone) Yes. Yes. (Switching)* Daddy!

DAD: Shhhhhh!

JESSIE: Damn it!

DAD: Please, Jessie. Twenty-one, thirty-four, fifty-five...

JESSIE: *(Into phone) Can you hold for one moment? (Pause)*
What do you want from me?

DAD: A Godless thing is hunting you, Jessie.

JESSIE: Daddy!

DAD: I captured this creature in Malaysia and brought
it home. Before your fifth birthday, the demon escaped.
Don't have to take on my burden. Understand? Eighty-
nine, a hundred forty-four, two hundred thirty-three...
I'm not allowed to say any more. Protect yourself.
Give me your hand...three hundred seventy-seven,
six hundred ten...

*(JESSIE returns to cell phone until she saunters back to table.
DAD eavesdrops on the following dialogue.)*

***

MOM: This is Jessie's friend...

FELIX: Felix.

BENNY: You look very familiar.

FELIX: Do I?

DAD: *(Only FELIX hears him.) You like to swim in open
waters. Nine hundred eighty-seven.*

FELIX: *(To BENNY)* No.

DAD: *(Only* FELIX *hears him.)* At night off the Coronado Bridge? One thousand five hundred ninety-seven.

MOM: Benny still mourns his departed wife.

JESSIE: *(On phone) Yes. Yes. It's easy to transcribe.*

BENNY: Missing over twenty-five years. She was my golden light.

JESSIE: *(Concluding call) Yes, I've release forms for each subject. They're all signed. Yes. I can turn everything in this week.*

(JESSIE *crosses back to the table.* DAD *saunters a few steps behind her.)*

MOM: Here's Jessie!

(FELIX *and* DAD *exchange looks. They can see each other.)*

BENNY: Your daughter knows my wife's spirit. She has her bracelet.

MOM: Your wife's bracelet?

BENNY: Yes, gold with a simple stone.

MOM: Did you give it to her?

BENNY: I did. The bracelet has memory.

MOM: Jessie, you look very upset.

(FELIX *discretely walks closer to* JESSIE.)

JESSIE: My school committee wants to crucify me. Four years of work. I can't believe it!

MOM: I'm so sorry, baby.

JESSIE: Everything is falling apart, Mom. Everything. Everything.

(CHANTELLE *approaches and everyone appears* quiet and dimly lit *except* JESSIE.)

CHANTELLE: *(Sings)*
Samantha flies to the jail bird,
Only you can make dear God heard.

JESSIE: *(Calmly to* MOM *and* FELIX*)* All week I keep
hearing Daddy's voice and a lost child's song.
Do you hear what I'm saying?

CHANTELLE: *(Change in tune.* CHANTELLE *caresses*
JESSIE's *hair.)* If that dog named Rover won't bark
Mama's gonna buy you a horse and cart
If that Horse and Cart fall down,
Then you'll be the sweetest little baby in town

JESSIE: I cannot fight my shine.

*(*CHANTELLE *kisses* JESSIE *on her cheek and then*
CHANTELLE *steps away from the table.)*

CHANTELLE: Samantha runs and runs all night.
Only you can make things right!

JESSIE: *(Disquiet in her calm voice)* I've felt two little girls
cry out in isolation. Someone must help them.

*(*CHANTELLE, *glowing, moves to the far end of the stage.*
The toyol's *light falls close to* JESSIE.*)*

JESSIE: Oh dear God!

(The sound of the toyol *is seductive rather than dreadful.)*

JESSIE: Please help me!

(The sound of babies crying drown out the toyol's *sound.)*

JESSIE: Something diabolical is taking over me....
(She doubles over with sharp abdominal pains.)

(End of scene)

END OF ACT ONE

ACT TWO

Scene Twenty-two

(JESSIE *and* FELIX *at the zoo's aviary. Sounds of many birds*)

JESSIE: This is one place guaranteed to cheer me up.
I used to love the wild birds at the zoo.

FELIX: They're not exactly wild here.

JESSIE: They don't know they're in captivity. But it's all an illusion.

FELIX: And what about you?

JESSIE: We're not in captivity, Felix.

FELIX: What are we then?

JESSIE: We're outsiders. Strange misfits.
Doctpr Ethnologist and Doctor Elevator.
Cover your damn head, that bird's about to shit.
(Pause) Too late.

(She wipes his head with a tissue.)

JESSIE: In Romania, bird poop means several days of romantic luck!

FELIX: But I'm struggling with my own private jinx.

JESSIE: Which is?

FELIX: The curse of failed intimacy.

JESSIE: There's a curse on the city's children...

FELIX: *(Completing her thought)* ...and it started with the Van Buren girl's murder.

JESSIE: *I could have been the Van Buren girl, Felix!*

FELIX: But you're not.

JESSIE: I see her, Felix. I hear her. She sings to me. Chantelle Van Buren's spirit won't rest until Samantha is found. I have to find them both or I'll go mad.

FELIX: I believe you. I know why you're obsessing about Chantelle. There's a boogieman in our own backyard.

JESSIE: David Winchester. Southeast of the Salton Sea. Calipatria State Prison. I've talked to the guards. I know where Samantha Shepard is. She was in my dream last night. Winchester talks to a child in shadow. I've secured an interview this week. Whether God is on my side or not, I'm going to face the devil with my bare hands. *(Pause)* You saw my father in the restaurant, didn't you?

FELIX: *(Reluctantly)* You're not going crazy. He's a walking ghost.

JESSIE: And you were keeping it a secret.

FELIX: I don't want any secrets between us anymore, Jessie. Your father is terrified.

JESSIE: Yes.

FELIX: And he has to wander like a tramp. I know you love him. Your father needs to find safe harbor. It's urgent, Jessie. He's punished himself for a very long time. He wants your love and absolution.

JESSIE: How do you know?

FELIX: I just know. Trust me. He's not allowed to ask for help.

JESSIE: How do you know?

FELIX: Because I'm just like him.

JESSIE: How are you like him?

FELIX: I swear to God!

JESSIE: Who did you hurt?

FELIX: My mother.

JESSIE: What did you do to her? Don't screw with my head, Felix.

FELIX: I'm not. The Bantu man told you about dispossessed bones. About spirits who wrestle with the realm of the living. And the Cambodian girl is preparing you to confront a *toyol*.

JESSIE: How the hell do you know these things?

FELIX: Your father adored you. Still adores you. He wants you to forget the past. He wants your heartfelt forgiveness, Jessie. Can I say it any plainer?

(He hugs her. She's in tears.)

FELIX: I'm falling. I'm falling, Jessie. Please. I love you, Jessie Gordon. Catch me.

JESSIE: What?

FELIX: Catch me with both arms. Please. We are Beauty and The Beast.

(End of scene)

Scene Twenty-three

(Campus office. A sign on the door: "Professor Blank, Department of Anthropology")

JESSIE: But some analogies are appropriate.

PROFESSOR: Really? The Chicano community is not like the Asian communities. The Native Americans are wholly unlike the East Africans.

JESSIE: You were the first to point out that funeral rituals were universal.

PROFESSOR: Jessie, there's a fine distinction between superstition and spiritualism. But even more appalling are these new chapters on Van Buren tragedy.

JESSIE: I'm not a sensationalist.

PROFESSOR: Your writing has taken on the rancid features of tabloid journalism. *(Reading)* "Megan's Law—named for a murdered girl—cannot stem the tide of child abductions. It is quite evident that our criminal courts are afraid to link the moral decadence in many homes with an open invitation to predators in our neighborhood. The systemic failure of detection and prevention *is transforming innocent children into macabre, ghostly apparitions.*" What the hell are you talking about?

JESSIE: Those are supplementary notes.

PROFESSOR: Supplementary notes to what? And this section on "fetuses in a jar"? "An Asian *toyol* can track a lost child from school or steal the toddler from family and friends. A blood red *toyol* can attack like a pit bull. A *toyol* is deaf to the cries and wails of our sons and daughters."

JESSIE: I know I'm digressing.

PROFESSOR: Digressing? Hell, you might as well do a moon walk on Pluto! Look, I'm your dissertation advisor, not your shrink. *(Conciliatory)* Your father helped me edit my first book. I was his protégé and his friend. He was very generous. Let's turn this thing around, Jessie. We'll rid all this voodoo crap from your writing. I owe you something.

JESSIE: Was my father psychic or psychotic?

PROFESSOR: Why ask that?

JESSIE: What did he really do in Malaysia?

PROFESSOR: It was so many years ago, Jessie.

JESSIE: I've found his hidden notebooks. Was he suspended from teaching?

PROFESSOR: He took an extended leave of absence.

JESSIE: You knew he brought back a *toyol.*

PROFESSOR: A *toyol*?

JESSIE: Did my father ask you to help me fight this thing? Tell me, damnit!

PROFESSOR: I'm not going to answer you, out of respect for his memory.

JESSIE: Tell me! Tell me the goddamn things he did in your presence!

PROFESSOR: Please, Jessie. You've no idea what you're getting into. That's all I can say.

JESSIE: Did it escape? Did the *toyol* kill my father?

PROFESSOR: Enough. For Christsake. Get out of my office.

(End of scene)

Scene Twenty-four

(Local children's playground. A dynamic little girl—played by the child actor portraying CHANTELLE—*leads a performance. The following nursery rhyme is supported by a taped chorus of children's voices, or* JESSIE *joining the girl as a make-shift chorus).*

*(*JESSIE *approaches and watches from the wings.)*

GIRL: *(With a pointer)* What are little boys made of?

CHORUS & GIRL: *What are little boys made of?*
Snips and snails
And puppy dogs tails
That's what little boys are made of!

GIRL: *(Seeing* JESSIE*)* Hi, we're singing to the angels!

JESSIE: I'm not an angel.

*(*GIRL *dances to herself.)*

JESSIE: I'm dreaming. I must be dreaming. I'm ovulating.

(Perhaps carousel music is heard.)

JESSIE: I'm standing on top of an unmarked grave.

GIRL: *(Smiling at* JESSIE*)* What are little girls made of?

GIRL/JESSIE:
What are little girls made of?
Sugar and spice,
And everything nice,
That's what little girls are made of!

*(*GIRL *dances to* JESSIE *and takes her hand.)*

GIRL: Hi Mommy!

JESSIE: I'm not your Mommy.

GIRL: Stay with me. Please!

(End of scene)

Scene Twenty-five

(Dream scene, hospital room. JESSIE *is on a bed, bathed in cool blue light. She is extremely cold.* HAMADI *and* QUEE *enter from opposite directions.)*

HAMADI: Wake up, Jessie.

QUEE: Wake up.

HAMADI: Wake up.

QUEE: Wake up, Jessie.

(Takes out a ksae—*a braided cord with a series of lead, copper or tin leaf squares, each separated by a knot.* QUEE *blows on each knot and recites a Cambodian mantra—endowing protective powers.)*

HAMADI: It's time to cool your father's bones. *(Unfurls a white fabric)*

QUEE: It's time to fight the *toyol*.

HAMADI: Who put you in the hospital?

QUEE: This *toyol* was sent by a condemned man.

HAMADI: Your father wanders.

QUEE: *(Points overhead)* The *toyol* is on the roof.

HAMADI: I brought you clean soil from my garden.

QUEE: *(Places the* ksae *around* JESSIE's *neck.)* You must wear this *ksae* to protect you from the hellish cold. Who's in the other bed, Jessie?

HAMADI: I also brought a clean lamb shank.

QUEE: A lamb can't fight a *toyol*!

HAMADI: This will bring your father to you.

QUEE: A crazy old tailor's coming.

HAMADI: *Princess*, please get out of bed!

QUEE: Remove all your make-up, Jessie. Even your mascara!

HAMADI: We take this bone from a lamb and we express our sorrow.

QUEE: In Cambodia, you try to trick the *toyol* with boiling oil!

HAMADI: Hold this warm bone. Cool the bone carefully.

QUEE: All clocks take the *toyol*'s side.

JESSIE: I'm so cold! My eyes hurt. Everything's blurry. I can't find my feet.

QUEE: One hundred thousand monarch butterflies circle overhead.

HAMADI: Hold the bone with an open hand.

QUEE: Still this demonic *toyol* moves closer for the hunt.

HAMADI: Point it skyward. I will help you.

QUEE: I will protect you.

BENNY: *(Carries his wife's golden dress)* I will follow you.

HAMADI: *Lil il-la-la.*

BENNY: Show me the way to find my wife.

QUEE: My father could kill this beast, but I can only coach you.

BENNY: I need you on the water, Jessie.

HAMADI: *Lil-il-la Mahumedu-rasuloola.*

BENNY: For you, I've a beautiful gown in rare gold.

QUEE: I'm G-2 and that's piss poor.

BENNY: My wife seeks your magic eye. Wear this. Protect the eye.

QUEE: Because you want to save children, the *toyol* will kill you.

(Acknowledging HAMADI and BENNY)

QUEE: Find your enemy.

HAMADI: And free your father.

BENNY: The moon is full, Jessie. Get up and fly!

JESSIE: *(Lifting up the bed sheet, she is horrified.)* Where are my legs!

HAMADI: *(To* BENNY*)* You took her legs away?

QUEE: *(With admiration addressed toward* BENNY*)*
The *toyol* tracks by the smell of her feet.

BENNY: *(Ignoring* HAMADI *and* QUEE *momentarily)*
You have wings, Jessie. Use them. Prove yourself.

(We hear the sound of the approaching toyol*.* HAMADI
and BENNY *vanish. Music)*

QUEE: Listen to me, Jessie.
You got to fight yourself
Inside and out, up and down
Kill yourself
Without bullshit
And accept all that you are.

(Music expands. QUEE *leads* JESSIE *in a* pas de deux *mixing
hip hop and Cambodian folk dance, teaching* JESSIE *how to
fight the* toyol*.* JESSIE *follows without fear.)*

QUEE: You have a shining power
To see all life invisible
Fear not things evil
Kill the *ordinary knowledge*
This is your only defense
Against the Asian creature.
I can't give you weapons
But you can make a shield.

(Gives her a small plate with broken mirrors)

QUEE: A small mirror won't kill it
But you can deflect the light.
Don't be a frightened deer.
Admit what you can.
Or else you die.

(Sound of the approaching toyol *grows louder)*

QUEE: Face this creature
And reverse the blinding light.

(The sound of the approaching toyol *grows deafening, overwhelming or mixing with* QUEE's *music.* QUEE *slaps* JESSIE *lightly on the head and vanishes. The* toyol *appears.* JESSIE *is alone with the creature. she circles the* toyol *several times carefully, slowly, fearfully. A sustained high pitch squeal is heard.* JESSIE *doubles up in pain. Her abdomen is attacked. She raises her hands above her head and howls. She "dances" with the mirrors reflecting the light, fighting the* toyol, *intuitively expanding upon what* QUEE *has taught her. at climax of the dance,* JESSIE *repels the* toyol *by crying out)*

JESSIE: Dear Jesus, Dead Jesus, Dear Jesus help me!

(She curls into a fetal position. an intern enters and covers her with a hospital gown)

(End of scene)

Scene Twenty-six

*(*JESSIE *is at her O B/G Y N.)*

DOCTOR: You don't sleep much, do you?

JESSIE: Graduate school, you know. Where's Doctor Brown?

DOCTOR: He was needed in the I C V unit. I'm his intern. Trina Richards. I know I look kind of young.

JESSIE: *(Pleasant kidding)* I was about to "card you".

DOCTOR: You've gained some weight.

JESSIE: Junk food. I'm addicted.

(They both laugh.)

DOCTOR: I'm the same way. I love Doritos and M & Ms—but Christ the acne! *(Pause)* Doctor Brown did blood and urine work the other day?

JESSIE: Yes.

DOCTOR: Your records mention abdominal pain.

JESSIE: Can you prescribe something for the horrible cramping?

DOCTOR: Sure. You're not doing recreational drugs, Jessie?

JESSIE: No.

DOCTOR: That will show up in the lab work.

JESSIE: I've smoked one joint in my entire life.

DOCTOR: Well, I wish I could say the same...but I can't.

(DOCTOR *picks up* JESSIE's *lab folder.*)

JESSIE: Believe me, I lead an unexciting life.

(Watching DOCTOR's *face)*

JESSIE: What is it?

DOCTOR: Hmmmmm, I've big news for you. *(Smiles)* I think it's very good news, but that's up to you.

JESSIE: Yes?

DOCTOR: You're pregnant, Jessie.

JESSIE: *WHAT?*

DOCTOR: That's right. *Mazel tov!*

JESSIE: No, no, no. I'm stunned!

DOCTOR: How late is your period?

JESSIE: I don't know.

DOCTOR: Don't you keep track of your calendar? I do. Well, it's time to be very aware of things now.

JESSIE: I'm sure you have someone else's file.

(DOCTOR *shakes head kindly.*)

JESSIE: Then run the tests again.

DOCTOR: Are you in a relationship?

JESSIE: *NO!*

DOCTOR: Okay. I understand. You're very independent.

JESSIE: You're nearly half my age.

DOCTOR: Do you want this child?

JESSIE: I haven't been sexually active in months.

DOCTOR: That's not what I asked.

JESSIE: What difference does it make?

DOCTOR: I'm trying to help you, Jessie.

JESSIE: I don't want your help.

DOCTOR: I don't need to know everything, Jessie, but let's deal with reality. There have been many inexplicable miscarriages in our county during the last six months. In fact that's what pulled Doctor Brown from his regular appointments today. Look, I want to ensure you have the best pre-natal care.

JESSIE: I can't be pregnant. And I'm not crazy. I'm not.

DOCTOR: No one is saying that you're unstable.

JESSIE: I'll go buy a goddamn twelve dollar take-home test and prove it!

DOCTOR: And prove what?

JESSIE: That you're wrong. You're not even twenty-five years old, for Christsakes!

DOCTOR: And if the store test shows I'm right?

JESSIE: Then I'm really losing my fucking mind.

(End of scene)

Scene Twenty-seven

(A figure in shadow uses an A T M machine. FELIX *and* DAD *meet.)*

DAD: One thousand five hundred ninety-seven. Two thousand five hundred eighty-four. Four thousand one hundred eighty-one. I think I forgot my PIN number.

FELIX: *(Preoccupied with his transaction)* What?

DAD: Do you have a PIN number?

FELIX: *(Looking at* DAD *for the first time in this scene)* Why do you need PIN number?

DAD: *(Takes out a cigarette and offers* FELIX *one)* I'm short cash this weekend.

FELIX: No thanks, I don't smoke anymore.

DAD: Won't kill you. Go ahead.

FELIX: *(Accepts cigarette. Awkward smile)* Thanks.

*(*DAD *can't get the lighter to work.)*

DAD: Got a match?

FELIX: Yeah...you and me?

DAD: I don't trust you. You found my daughter in the nick of time.

FELIX: That's true. But my intentions are pure.

DAD: What are your intentions?

FELIX: To marry Jessie.

DAD: Wonderful. I'm going. You're staying. For Christsake, I'm jealous. *(Pause)* My daughter needs protection. You know I'm very serious.

FELIX: I'll do what I can.

DAD: That's not good enough.

FELIX: I'm not Superman.

DAD: I didn't ask you to put on a red cape and boots.

FELIX: I know.

DAD: But you know what's hunting her?

FELIX: I do. You know I can't kill it, but I can shield her.

DAD: Good.

FELIX: I love Jessie. I'll die for her if that's what it takes.

DAD: That's what it might take.

(End of scene)

Scene Twenty-eight

(JESSIE at her father's cemetery. She stands, with HAMADI's lamb shank, by his grave stone. A long buttoned coat hides the gold gown worn under the coat.)

JESSIE: Goddamn it, I'm so cold. Day or night. Please understand. *(Performs a simple movement with the shank and then places the bone on the ground)* Daddy. Don't make me go insane! Please help me. My childhood was desecrated. When you died, I wanted to die. You abandoned me *twice*. When you left me with Uncle Teddy and when you took your life. Still, Hell is not your home. *(Pause)* How the fuck did I get pregnant? Why is this *toyol* stalking me? Did it really kill you? Can I trust Felix? What causes a murdered girl to haunt me so? *(Pause)* When I see you next, Daddy, I will kiss you and I will hug you. I will cherish you until my dying day. *(Pause)* You were only fifty seven when you took your life, and we were just starting to have the best, real conversations and you began to admire my mind.

(FELIX approaches, but she doesn't see him yet.)

JESSIE: When you talk to me again, do it here where it is safe and sacred. Not anywhere else.
Please. I beg you. Please, Daddy. I don't want to go crazy. And I am going crazy.
You never left a note for me. Did you leave because you hated our family?
Did you lose all sense of reality? Is that happening to me, Daddy? *(Pause)* If you're *not* in God's good graces, I hope God reconsiders. *That really is my prayer.*
I believe God loves you dearly. Daddy, I forgive you.
I dearly love you. Please be restless no more

FELIX: *(Softly)* Your father's an exceptional man.

JESSIE: *(Startled)* Felix?

FELIX: I had to follow you here.

JESSIE: Why?

FELIX: I'm running out of time. Jess, I dream about you day and night. Very personal dreams.

JESSIE: Where are your parents, Felix? A real person has parents, family, roots...

FELIX: I told you, my Mom's dead. Pop's a prick and lives in Dallas. No siblings.

JESSIE: Did you go to your Mom's funeral?

FELIX: Yes, and cried like a little boy.

JESSIE: Something supernatural is trailing me.

FELIX: I know.

JESSIE: And I have to fight it with everything I got.

FELIX: I can't kill it, Jess. But I'll die for you.

JESSIE: I don't want you to die, you idiot.

(He nods coolly.)

JESSIE: I'm pregnant. I'm serious. My doctor told me Tuesday...

FELIX: Oh shit! Oh Good God, Jesus, Mary and Joseph! That's wonderful news, Jess!

JESSIE: Don't say that. It's miserable news. Goddamn crazy news. I don't know how the hell this happened.

FELIX: Who gives a fuck! I think it's great news.

JESSIE: I'm freaking out. I haven't slept with you. I haven't slept with any guy in over a year.

FELIX: You're scared?

(Shakes her head again)

FELIX: You're very scared. I love you with all my heart and soul, Jessie.

(She cries. He puts his arm around her.)

(End of scene)

Scene Twenty-nine

(School yard and JESSIE's *bedroom.* WINCHESTER *and* SAMANTHA *are on a see-saw in his cell, while* JESSIE, *in terry robe, is awoken by her father.)*

WINCHESTER: When I'm up, you're down.

SAMANTHA: You be the princess.

WINCHESTER: You be the witch.

SAMANTHA: When I'm up, you're down.

DAD: One, one, three, five, eight, thirteen...

JESSIE: *(Half awake)* Dad?

DAD: Mom and I eloped.

JESSIE: What??

WINCHESTER: You be the song.

SAMANTHA: You be the dance.

WINCHESTER: When I'm up, you're down.

SAMANTHA: You be the girl.

WINCHESTER: You be the boogeyman.

DAD: Jessie, you deserve a large wedding. Before another tragedy hits home. *(Pause)* Thirteen, twenty-one, thirty-four, fifty-five...I had planned a summer-long vacation with you. But I was obsessed with an illegal study in Kuala Lumpar. Don't fall asleep, Jessie! And then came a breakthrough with *toyols*. And a child prostitution ring in Asia. Do you understand?

JESSIE: I was four years old.

SAMANTHA: Boooooooooooooo!

WINCHESTER: Boooooooooooooooooooooo!!

SAMANTHA: Boooo!

WINCHESTER: Boo!!

(They do a little dance as they continue to chant boo, boo, boo.)

DAD: I exposed an entire racketeering group.

JESSIE: I was four years old, Daddy.

DAD: I captured the *toyols* and secured it under lock and key. It was vital to study every living cell of this demon. But a campus janitor knocked over the jar. The thing escaped.

WINCHESTER/SAMANTHA: Booo! Booo! Booo!

(WINCHESTER teachers SAMANTHA a song.)

WINCHESTER: Hush, little baby, don't say a word
Mama's gonna buy you a mockin'bird.

DAD: I wanted to kill my brother. And all those years which followed could not lessen my guilt, Jessie. Listen, carefully!

(Pause. She removes terry robe and we see the gold gown given to her by BENNY*)*

DAD: Eighty-nine, one hundred fifty-one, two hundred forty-three, three hundred ninety-seven... You're now a target for this hateful *toyol*. Because you're my daughter. Do you understand? You must fight. *Destroying the nest or the nest is paramount.* You must face the master. Turn the creature against the master. Shield your eyes. Pray with heart and soul, *and don't watch the* toyol *surprise his master, dear Jesus!*

SAMANTHA: Hush, little baby, don't say a word

WINCHESTER: If that mockin' bird don't sing Mama's gonna buy you a diamond ring

SAMANTHA: Mama's gonna buy you a diamond ring.

(End of scene)

Scene Thirty

*(*JESSIE *and* BENNY *are at the carousel at seaport village. We hear the music of the carousel which is a medley of standard carousel, but then transforms into* BENNY'*s wife's song.* JESSIE *is wearing* BENNY'*s wife's dress.)*

JESSIE: Do you hear that?

BENNY: What?

JESSIE: Your wife singing?

BENNY: I was never here.

JESSIE: Too many tourists.

BENNY: Yes.

JESSIE: Seaport Village was built in the late 1970s. The waterfront was urban blight.

BENNY: You think she's here? *(He picks up some soil from the nearby flower bed.)*

JESSIE: I hear her voice singing. In this direction. Please. *(Pause)* She was selling food to the construction workers during ground breaking. I hear her vividly In this park.

BENNY: But are you sure?

JESSIE: Yes.

BENNY: My wife. My dear lost wife. She is nearby?

JESSIE: She's very close. It's so distinct.

(BENNY *sings or hums his wife's song*)

JESSIE: She's here. You'll have to notify the Indian Authorities for permission in order to unearth her remains.

BENNY: No, all I need is my shovel in the car. *(Exits)*

JESSIE: Benny, Benny!

(End of scene)

Scene Thirty-one

(JESSIE and MOM are at the IHOP. Under JESSIE's coat, we can see BENNY'S gold gown—shining as if brand new. the coat comes off sometime during the scene.)

MOM: Talk to me, sweetheart.

JESSIE: I feel like I'm terribly lost.

MOM: What happened?

JESSIE: Something monstrous is stalking me.

MOM: That guy?

JESSIE: No, it's the same thing that went after Daddy. Cold light spills into the bedroom window at night. I'm freezing all the time.

MOM: What happened to Daddy was medically preventable.

JESSIE: You think I'm delusional.

MOM: You're not delusional. But I'm deeply worried about your physical condition.

JESSIE: But I'm haunted by impossible things.

(Sensing she's hit a wall with her MOM*)*

JESSIE: Mom, Felix wants to get very serious.

(Restrained, MOM *nods supportively.)*

JESSIE: Listen please, I love him. But I paid for one of the internet background searches. I got back a very long, upsetting report.

MOM: What did it say? *(Silence)* Is he already married?

JESSIE: No.

MOM: What? D W I? A felon who broke parole?

JESSIE: No.

MOM: A former priest-sex offender who went on Judge Judy? *(Pause)* What did it report!

JESSIE: Felix was a science student at S D S U who dropped out in his senior year, despite a 4.0 G P A. He served in the navy. Received a dishonorable discharge.

MOM: So he's a flaming homosexual.

JESSIE: No liens against him. No criminal record, a few library fines. Born in El Paso, 1975. He comes from a small family who moved to San Diego in the early 1990s. He was employed by the city as an elevator inspector for two years, before quitting his job.

MOM: All that from the internet?

JESSIE: There's more.

MOM: He's homosexual.

JESSIE: At S D S U he was a computer hacker. He got into a lot of student files. The school never pressed charges.

MOM: And his medical profile? Any diseases?

JESSIE: Nothing on record. He's never been fingerprinted.

MOM: Are you satisfied now?

JESSIE: No.

MOM: Why not?

JESSIE: According to the report and eyewitness accounts, Felix jumped off the Coronado bridge in October 2004.

MOM: *(Somewhat muted)* Oh really?

JESSIE: Did you hear what I just said?

MOM: Yes. You said he jumped. Many unhappy homosexuals jump off that bridge.

JESSIE: Everyone dies off that bridge! It's a two hundred foot drop.

MOM: I guess it depends on what you're wearing that day, Jessie.

JESSIE: Mom, you're infuriating!

MOM: Darling, you're telling me really bizarre things that you got from a late night printout.

JESSIE: His body wasn't found in the water

MOM: Because he's walking around today.

JESSIE: It was assumed that *he died that day* according to the police report.

MOM: Well, obviously he didn't die. Lucky you!

JESSIE: Is that sarcasm?

MOM: *Moi?*

JESSIE: I'm very upset.

MOM: You should be. Better talk to the police.

JESSIE: And say what?

MOM: That lover boy was a jumper and probably collected on his own insurance policy.

JESSIE: I can't do that.

MOM: I'll make the call!

JESSIE: No.

MOM: I'm concerned about your safety, Jessie.

JESSIE: I'll just ask him.

MOM: How crazy are you!

JESSIE: What?

MOM: Don't do that.

JESSIE: Why not?

MOM: He'll know that you've been checking on him. And then what?

JESSIE: I'll take that risk.

MOM: Why do you think he jumped?

JESSIE: Why did Daddy hang himself?

MOM: Don't compare this nitwit to your father!

JESSIE: Goddamn it, why can't you ever hear me!

MOM: I hear you loud and clear.

JESSIE: Are you getting serious with Benny?

MOM: What has that to do with you?

JESSIE: Then you are getting serious with him. What do you think Dad would say about that?

MOM: I really don't know. Daddy would want me to be happy, Jessie. I wish you could understand my real needs.

(End of scene)

Scene Thirty-two

(Night. in front of carousel at seaport village. BENNY, alone, has brought burning sweet grass or sage, a plate of his wife's favorite food, a red cloth, a photo or effigy of his wife made from a stick wrapped in leather and beads, a disk of shell, live coals and other gifts for his wife. As he chants and prays the text below he performs a burial ritual: he cleans his hands with bottled water. He purifies his hands and food with the smoke of sweet grass or sage. He holds the food above the grave site, asking for blessing in his native language. BENNY buries food in the ground, covers grave with the cloth and lays the photo, effigy, shell and gifts for his wife on the grave. During the ceremony, Phyllis arrives and watches carefully.)

BENNY: In my sadness I know you smile in peace.
In my sorrow I know you remail true.
In my heart I feel the hills of time.
In my soul I am free to hold you once again.
In peace, in truth, through the canyons of time.
You were my first wife and I young again no more.
Young again no more.
Our children run
And I must walk
Older than years and years and years.
(Completing the ritual)
Now she has a proper grave.

MOM: *(Not seeing BENNY's face yet)* Yes.

BENNY: My wife thought this waterfront land, *La Punta*, was part of her family tribe. She believed her grandparents died here. *La Punta.* I understand why she found her way here in her innocence. *(Pause)* We have consecrated the earth and have purified her memory. (BENNY *turns and removes his hat for the first time in the play. His long gray hair flows down and he has aged twenty five years—looks sixty five.)*

BENNY: *(Sings. Phyllis may join in the final phrases of the song)* She kissed me under a black cloud
And the heavy sky turned bright
The cold wind broke through so loud
Song birds and eagles fell from sight
How can you love a spirit, she asked.
In song, I said.
In song, I said.
How can you marry a spirit, she asked.
In song, I said.
In song, I said.
We dance, We cling
We sleep, We sing.

MOM: *(Aware of* BENNY'*s aging)* Oh my dear Lord... are you all right...Benny?

BENNY: Yes. Thank you, Phyllis. This is who I am and your daughter was the powerful search light. *(Tenderly)* I want to tell you my tribal name. It is Eye Hop. Yes, Eye Hop. *(He points to his eye in a soft moment of humor.)* This is true, little flower. And I love you more than a young man in springtime.

(End of scene)

Scene Thirty-three

(JESSIE *and* FELIX *on foot along the Coronado Bridge.*
Their car broke down midway on the bridge.)

JESSIE: I had the car serviced two weeks ago.

FELIX: Wonderful.

JESSIE: Keep walking. We'll get a cab on the other side
of the bridge.

FELIX: Not with this luck. You know it's illegal to cross
this bridge on foot.

JESSIE: I was able to reserve room 3312 at the Hotel del
Coronado.

FELIX: Kate Morgan's room?

JESSIE: Yes. Two months to get the damn reservation.
Great view of the harbor!
You know the Kate Morgan story?

(They stop walking. Prompts him)

JESSIE: Love suicide in the hotel.

FELIX: Or hotel abortion. November 1892. She worked
a gambling con. Hundreds of guys were fleeced at
the card table. Kate was gorgeous. Had a surprise
pregnancy which flipped out her husband.

JESSIE: Kate's husband knew the baby wasn't his.

FELIX: She was found dead with quinine by her bed.
Her motive was abortion, not suicide.

JESSIE: The cops claimed she bought a .44 caliber.
A small bullet mark to her head, blood everywhere.
The bullet didn't match her gun.

FELIX: And they never found her killer. Are we staying
the night?

JESSIE: Yes.

FELIX: What about the car?

JESSIE: Screw the car. I'll get it towed.

FELIX: You want to sleep with me?

JESSIE: Are you afraid?

(They continue to walk.)

JESSIE: The room has two beds. One for dreamers. The other for the schemers. Which one are you?

FELIX: I know how to dream.

JESSIE: I had a dream last night about you. You were in a rental car going to Coronado. It was a very bad dream.

(They stop walking again.)

JESSIE: You left the car on the bridge. Hard rain falling. You climbed over the railing and jumped.

FELIX: *That wasn't a goddamn dream!*

JESSIE: I know, Felix. There are no coincidences. Tell me the truth. I was also on that bridge that night! I remember the police cars.

FELIX: *(Realizing for the first time)* I saw your face. I saw your eyes. You stopped your car. There was a police helicopter.

JESSIE: I couldn't see your face because of the flood lights. I screamed.

FELIX: I never hit the water. I've one more chance at life! You saved me.

JESSIE: Did you jump?

FELIX: Help me, Jess!

JESSIE: Tell the truth.

FELIX: I had no one. Nothing was holding me back. No hand, no love, no woman. I had to jump.

JESSIE: But you lived, Felix.

FELIX: No one survives this damn bridge. *(He clings to bridge rail as if to straddle it.)*

JESSIE: Felix. You're not going to jump a second time. I couldn't stop my father from suicide, but I can stop you.

FELIX: It's not up to me.

JESSIE: *(She touches him.)* Yes, it is.

FELIX: I don't deserve you, Jess. *(He straddles bridge rail with his legs.)*

JESSIE: Damn it!

(She yanks him back to the secure side of the railing.)

FELIX: Look at the cursed souls leaping out of desperation. Like insects

JESSIE: I love you, you idiot!

(He falls into her arms.)

FELIX: Dear God Almighty...

(She kisses him longingly.)

JESSIE: Are you a ghost?

FELIX: No, but you're my guardian angel.

JESSIE: I want you *if you're real.*

FELIX: I'm real!

JESSIE: Are you the father of my baby?

FELIX: I don't know. I really don't know. I shouldn't even be alive,

JESSIE: Answer me!

FELIX: We never really made love, Jessie.

JESSIE: Are you the father of my baby!

FELIX: *I would like to be.*

(She hits him on the arm.)

FELIX: I *could be* the father of your baby.
And your lawful husband if you would let me.
I love you more than life itself.

(End of scene)

Scene Thirty-four

*(*JESSIE *interviews* WINCHESTER *in prison. Midway into the scene the little girl* SAMANTHA *will appear to* WINCHESTER *and* JESSIE. WINCHESTER *hides his discomfort caused by the girl's presence.* JESSIE *wears a man's baseball cap.* WINCHESTER *wears manacles on his feet and hands.* CHANTELLE's *presence is part of this scene too.)*

SAMANTHA: *(Loud whisper, far away from* WINCHESTER*)*
Teddy bear, Teddy bear
Show your shoe
Teddy bear, Teddy bear
That will do.
Teddy bear, Teddy bear
Run upstairs
Teddy bear, Teddy bear
Say your prayers

WINCHESTER: No taping, nor note-taking. You only have five minutes.

JESSIE: You promised an hour.

WINCHESTER: ...not another second more.

JESSIE: May I begin?

WINCHESTER: Where did you get my cap?

JESSIE: The guard sold it to me for seventy-five dollars.
I like souvenirs. *(Pause)* Do you feel you received a fair
trial?

WINCHESTER: The case was tried in public before
getting to the courthouse. Do I frighten you?

(JESSIE, having trouble seeing, squints. the invisible toyol
growls at her.)

WINCHESTER: You're squinting

(SAMANTHA approaches him.)

WINCHESTER: Is the light blinding you?

JESSIE: Do you believe in God, Mister Winchester?

WINCHESTER: God is a canker sore.

(More intense light from the toyol)

JESSIE: Do you believe in an afterlife?

WINCHESTER: I don't. Do you?

(SAMANTHA approaches WINCHESTER.)

JESSIE: Do you believe ghosts exist?

WINCHESTER: I look like your uncle. Shut your eyes.
He walked with a limp.

JESSIE: *(Bracing herself)* Do you ever see or talk to ghosts?

WINCHESTER: Maybe in my dreams. And I've mastered
the art of grooming my *toyol*. What was you uncle like?
(Pause) Come closer.

JESSIE: He raced Italian sports cars and he was a world
class shit. *(Cupping her eyes with her hand)* Do you think
Chantelle's spirit is restless?

WINCHESTER: No.

JESSIE: She has never visited you in this prison?

WINCHESTER: What an asinine question! Sweet Chantelle has left the earth.

JESSIE: No girl has come to you here?

WINCHESTER: Only big girls like you. Do you like older men more than ice cream?

JESSIE: *(Trying to keep her eyes on him)* Are you atoning for your actions which brought you here?

(He offers a reptilian smile.)

JESSIE: I don't like older men. Have you atoned?

WINCHESTER:
Atoned? I have cried more than most men.
Believe me, I am an innocent, injured man.
What happened in court was a travesty of justice.
(Pause) Yet I am truly sorry for the tragedy which befell the Van Buren family and I wish I could turn back the hands of time.

JESSIE: You think the parents were negligent?

WINCHESTER: Was your father negligent?

JESSIE: Have you regrets about anything that you've done?

WINCHESTER: I was stupid to be friendly to my neighbors, wrong to dance with slutty, inebriated, married women, wrong to download kiddie porn, and...

JESSIE: And? *(She wipes her face.)*

WINCHESTER: And many upstanding adults are just like me... All little girls are gracious. All children are angels. And the Devil made sport of me. *(Looks at his watch)* You're pregnant, aren't you? Hormones driving you nuts? *(Pause)* High cortisol levels are causing you vision problems.

(The toyol's *light approaches* JESSIE.*)*

JESSIE: *(Collecting her papers to leave)* Thank you for your time.

WINCHESTER: Your first baby.

JESSIE: How do you know these things?

WINCHESTER: Satan has my soul. Look at me.

JESSIE: Yes, Satan has your soul and that is a tragedy.

WINCHESTER: You're in my undisguised dreams.
And in my dreams I am allowed to know everything.

JESSIE: I'm done with my interview. *(Feeling very faint)*

WINCHESTER: Keep the baby, my little angel.

JESSIE: So he can run into a creature like you?

WINCHESTER: I'm no harm to any child here.

JESSIE: Thank God.

WINCHESTER: And go tell that shadow of a boyfriend that he's run out of time. Avoid tunnels and bridges. He's a jumper, my flower.

JESSIE: Since you know so many secrets, tell me one of yours. *(Shying away from the* toyol's *light)*

WINCHESTER: Tell you?

JESSIE: Yes. *(Takes off* WINCHESTER's *baseball cap)*

WINCHESTER: Are you pretending we're in a fairy tale?

JESSIE: Yes, and you're the troll at the bridge.

WINCHESTER: I like that. I'm the troll! All right then. You have to guess.

JESSIE: There's a little girl under five years old who visits. She's crossed a bridge but she's lost.

SAMANTHA: He gives me little gifts and special treats.

JESSIE: The guards can't see her, but you do.

SAMANTHA: Don't hurt him.

JESSIE: She's standing right next to you. And she has one more chance to come back home.

(*Without seeing her,* JESSIE *points at* SAMANTHA, *who stands between* JESSIE *and the* toyol)

WINCHESTER: Go to hell!

JESSIE: Her name is Samantha.

(*The* toyol *growls.*)

WINCHESTER: Guards!

JESSIE: Samantha...go home. I'm telling you that you can now go home. This man is very sick. He is sick. Please go home. Your parents need you. They love you. Go home, Samantha!

(CHANTELLE *joins the scene from a safe distance.*)

WINCHESTER: Don't listen to her, Samantha! She's a witch. I am your best friend.

JESSIE: Go home, Samantha. You know the way home. Mommy and Daddy are waiting.

(SAMANTHA *starts to leave and* WINCHESTER *manages to grab her.*)

JESSIE: Let her go! I said—*let her go!*
I'll kill you, Winchester. (*She uses a mirror to reflect* toyol*'s light in his direction.*) Dear God, please help her. Please. Please help.

(*The* toyol*'s light and sound intensifies on* WINCHESTER.)

WINCHESTER: (*Holds* SAMANTHA) You must understand. This darling child cannot be sent home! She still lives with me. She's my great love!

(JESSIE *directs more light and sound at* WINCHESTER.)

WINCHESTER: My eyes!

(SAMANTHA *breaks free of his grip.*)

WINCHESTER: Samantha! Don't leave me! I'm not the boogeyman. There is no boogeyman. There is only the Holy Ghost suspended between Paradise and the great fires.

(JESSIE *directs climactic shaft of light at him.*)

WINCHESTER: My eyes!

(SAMANTHA *begins to exit.*)

WINCHESTER: Hold me, Jessie. I'm your father's sad older brother haunting Cuyamaca Park.

(*The* toyol *blinds* WINCHESTER *with a shaft of brilliant light. He groans quietly in agony*)

WINCHESTER: Christ, my soul! Help me!

(SAMANTHA *exits.*)

JESSIE: No. I win, you lose.

(*Her eyesight is better.* CHANTELLE *approaches* WINCHESTER.)

CHANTELLE: (*Sings to* WINCHESTER)
Hush, little baby, don't say a word
Mama's gonna buy you a mockin'bird.

(*She touches his shoulders on the last sung word.* WINCHESTER *falls and collapses to the floor*)

CHANTELLE: And if that mockin'bird don't sing...

(WINCHESTER *utters a gutteral scream.* JESSIE *steps toward the toyol in the jar. She lifts the jar with both hands and smashes it to the floor. a flood of white light in every direction.*)

CHANTELLE: Mama's gonna buy you a diamond ring. (*She smiles in triumph.*)

(*End of scene*)

Scene Thirty-five

(JESSIE *on the Coronado Bridge*)

JESSIE: Two weeks after Halloween, all the odd
symptoms of autism faded from the local schools.
It was as if a pied piper brought the children together
for healing in one magnificent processional. Chantelle
ascended to Heaven and Samantha returned to the land
of the living. And that is the bittersweet, unfiltered
truth. *(Pause)* Just before Thanksgiving, I stopped
work. I threw all my committee notes into the ocean.
(She tosses her committee notes over the rail) Those early
chapters were for a dissertation that misled me
miserably. I kissed my new book and mailed it to
Random House. I did not need the PhD anymore.
(Pause) I was no longer estranged. I accepted this gift
that I inherited. I would have *the shine* all my natural
living days. My father was right. I was in love. *(Pause)*
I counted out the seasons. I counted out each grain of
sand. I would go into labor early May. May Day. May
Day. What a lovely sound. Felix is my beloved. And we
both have a second chance at life. *(Pause)* Every flower
is temporal. Life begins with love. And sex. And birth.
And death.

*(jessie's father enters and he dances softly with her to a 1950s
Sinatra ballad—Only the Lonely. FELIX enters in stylish
tux with gift box which he places on nighttable. FELIX "cuts
in' to dance with JESSIE. JESSIE's father exits and in crossing
is joined by CHANTELLE into the darkness. lights fade to
black.)*

(End of scene)

Scene Thirty-six

(Change of time and space. Kate Morgan's room at the Hotel del Coronado. FELIX *and* JESSIE *continue to dance. During the scene* JESSIE *will open the gift box revealing a silk kimono.* FELIX *helps her put on the garment.)*

JESSIE: Are we good for each other?

FELIX: Yes.

JESSIE: Should I believe you?

FELIX: Yes.

JESSIE: Are you a ghost?

FELIX: No. Not any more.

JESSIE: Will our child be a special?

FELIX: Indeed.

JESSIE: There's a deck of cards on the night table. Did you bring them? *(Pause)* Are the cards marked, Felix? *(Pause)* Are you making the cards move?

FELIX: You said the room was haunted by Kate Morgan. She was ambivalent about her pregnancy.

JESSIE: Yes.

FELIX: But you're not.

JESSIE: I want the baby. Kate Morgan was a con artist.

FELIX: You're not.

JESSIE: No.

FELIX: Will you marry me?

JESSIE: Will I marry you?

FELIX: Yes.

JESSIE: When?

FELIX: Tomorrow. We'll go to City Hall.

JESSIE: Pick up the deck of cards, Felix.

FELIX: Why?

JESSIE: If you draw hearts, I'll know exactly what to do.

FELIX: I can't touch the cards. They were meant for you.

JESSIE: Pick up the cards. *(Reluctant he picks up the cards)* Concentrate.

FELIX: This is so silly, Jessie

(Cards fly out of his jacket sleeves. She picks up a few from the floor. They are all cards with hearts on them.)

JESSIE: All hearts, Felix. All beautiful fresh hearts! A thousand brilliant, red hearts! *(A beautiful shower of playing cards or rose petals comes from the rafters. Lights change.)*

(End of scene)

Epilogue

(A jump of time, four or five years later. a scene in the school yard with several school. we see one child surrounded by childlike puppets, or stuffed animals. JESSIE and FELIX enter the yard, followed by MOM and BENNY who uses a cane now, then HAMADI and QUEE enter. on the large screen we see photos of HAMADI's son, QUEE's father, BENNY's wife and JESSIE's DAD.)

GIRL: My darling teddy bears.
Come out, come out
And drop your silly fears
(She dances in simple circle.)
Teddy bear, Teddy bear
Touch the ground

Teddy bear, Teddy bear
Turn around
Teddy bear, Teddy bear,
Blow out the light
(Pause)
Teddy bear, Teddy bear,
Say good night.

(Lights pull in GIRL *and* JESSIE, *as they walk towards each other.)*

JESSIE: In a blink of an eye my baby grew up.
My glorious four year old angel.

JESSIE/GIRL: *(Singing)*
Nighttime is coming early
I don't even seen the moon
Pajamas will make me girly
Dark has come too soon
Now the little ones get tired
And need to rest their eyes
So be still and sit beside me
For our lullabies
(They kiss.)

GIRL: Teddy bear, Teddy bear,
Say good night.
Good night
Good night
and don't let
the bedbugs bite.

END OF PLAY

www.ingramcontent.com/pod-product-compliance
Lightning Source LLC
Chambersburg PA
CBHW052139090426
42741CB00009B/2148